Published 2017 by North Parade Publishing Ltd.
4 North Parade, Bath, England.
www.nppbooks.co.uk

Printed in China

THE COMPLETE
ILLUSTRATED
CHILDREN'S
BIBLE
ATLAS

npp

nppbooks.co.uk

NorthParadePublishing

Maps

Contents

Introduction

The Bible is full of great journeys and exotic-sounding place names. Without an in-depth knowledge of the landscape of ancient times, it can be difficult to visualize these locations and to understand how monumental some of the journeys were. The better you understand the lands of the Bible, the better you will understand the Bible itself.

The Bible follows the story of the Jewish people—their relationship with God, but also their relationship with the land, for their history was bound to the land. Maps help us both to envision and to understand the impact of physical barriers, such as lakes, seas, mountains, rivers, and deserts. It's clear the landscape played an important role in the story of the Bible. Important trade routes are the source of conflict and friction, and fertile land is always fought over—particularly significant, because Canaan, the Promised Land, was in the Fertile Crescent (an arc of land cultivated by the Tigris and the Euphrates rivers). When God tells Abraham to leave his comfortable, fertile home and to go to the land of Canaan, promising that he would make him the father of a great nation, it may be hard to immediately grasp why Canaan is so important. But maps can help us see that it was right in the heart of the ancient world, at the meeting point of three enormous land masses—Asia, Africa, and Europe. With the Mediterranean sea to the west, and all the prosperity and opportunity that that offered, and the inhospitable desert to the east, Canaan was an important trading route linking Egypt and the city-states of Mesopotamia, and of immense strategic value. When you look at the position of Canaan on a map, all this becomes very clear.

Besides this, it is wonderful to see the actual location of places we have heard so much about. Jesus was born in Bethlehem, raised in Nazareth, and baptized in the river Jordan. He preached by the Sea of Galilee and was crucified in Jerusalem. The Bible becomes more real, looking at these places on a map.

In addition to this, we are able to conceive of the length and distance of the journeys depicted in the Bible so much better when looking at a physical representation of them. Adam and Eve migrate east following their expulsion from the Garden of Eden, which is widely regarded as being located in Mesopotamia. Abraham leaves his home in Ur, at one end of the Fertile Crescent in Mesopotamia, to travel to Canaan, at the other end. His great-grandson Joseph is sold into slavery and taken from Canaan to Egypt, where he becomes second in command to Pharaoh himself, later being joined by his father Jacob and the rest of their people. The Hebrew people spend many years enslaved in Egypt before being led out by Moses, who takes them on a slow and arduous journey through the wilderness (the barren and unforgiving Sinai Desert) back to the Promised Land of Canaan, although Moses himself only sees the land from the slopes of Mount Nebo.

The relationship between the Jewish people and their home in Canaan is of central importance to the Bible. When they originally settled in the area, they slowly conquered cities and territories, dividing the land up among themselves. Under the rule of King Saul, the twelve tribes of Israel were united into one nation. King David made Jerusalem the capital city for that nation, and during the reign of his son, King Solomon, the first temple was built in the city.

Any stability is short-lived, and soon the land becomes divided into Israel in the north and Judah in the south. It also comes under threat from a number of opposing nations: the Assyrians, the Philistines, and finally the mighty Babylonians. Both Judah and the city of Jerusalem fall to Babylonia, and many of the Israelites find themselves in exile. In time, with the Persian conquest of Babylon, the Jews are permitted to return to their homeland and begin the slow process of rebuilding their city and temple.

When we begin the New Testament, the Roman Empire holds sway over the land. Because of the census ordered by the Roman emperor, Mary travels with Joseph to Bethlehem to register, and there she gives birth to Jesus. Mary and Joseph later flee with Jesus to Egypt, but later they return to Nazareth, their hometown, where Jesus grows up. After the crucifixion and the resurrection, we follow the travels of some of Jesus' disciples, in particular those of the apostle Paul, who journeys far and wide to lands including Greece and Asia Minor to preach the good news. Imprisoned in Rome toward the end of his life, Paul still continues to send his letters of instruction, correction, and hope to the fledgling churches in Asia. The Bible ends with the book of Revelation, written on the Greek island of Patmos, where the author, John, has an incredible vision of the end of days.

The Bible covers a variety of locations both familiar and unfamiliar to us, which provide more than just a backdrop to the events depicted—the landscape plays a vital role in the Bible story. Clearly it is crucial for us to understand the world that hugely important figures like Jesus, Abraham, Jacob, and Paul lived in.

John on the island of Patmos. In his vision he was shown the end of days, and then a new heaven and earth and the Holy City, shining with the glory of God.

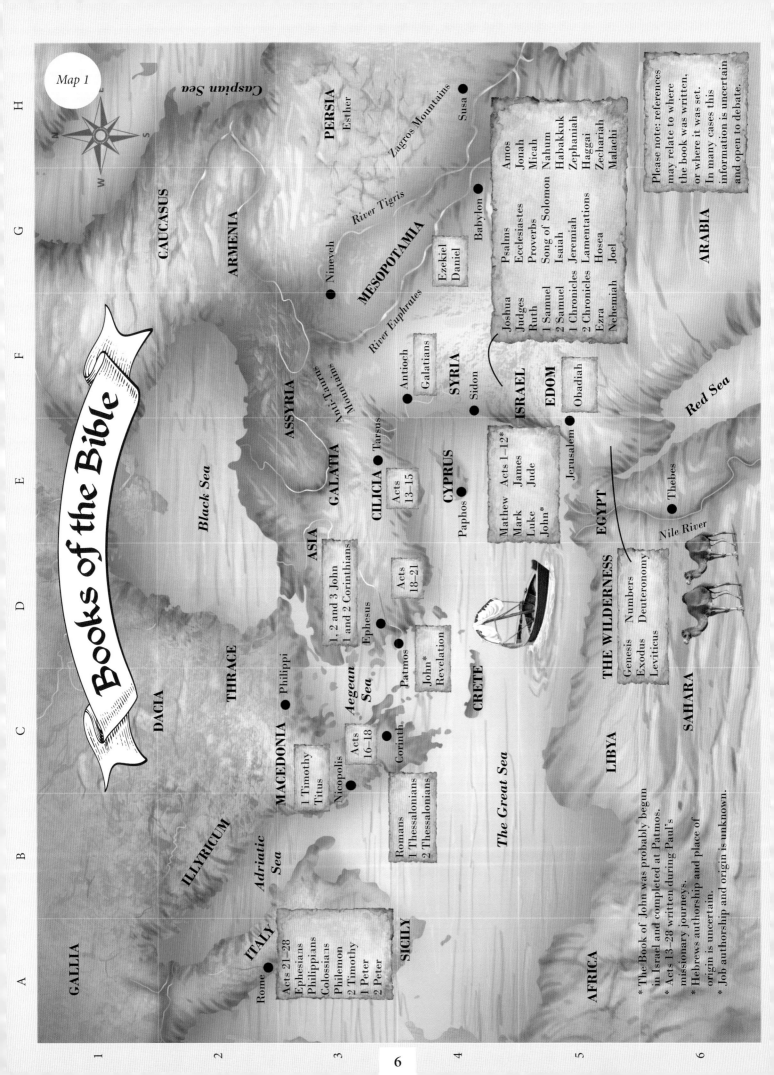

Map 1

Books of the Bible

Please note: references may relate to where the book was written, or where it was set. In many cases this information is uncertain and open to debate.

GALLIA

ITALY
Rome

Acts 21–28
Ephesians
Philippians
Colossians
Philemon
2 Timothy
1 Peter
2 Peter

ILLYRICUM

Adriatic Sea

DACIA

THRACE

MACEDONIA
Philippi

1 Timothy
Titus

Nicopolis

Acts 16–18

Corinth

Romans
1 Thessalonians
2 Thessalonians

SICILY

ASIA

1, 2 and 3 John
1 and 2 Corinthians

Ephesus

Patmos

John*
Revelation

Acts 18–21

CRETE

Aegean Sea

The Great Sea

AFRICA

LIBYA

SAHARA

Black Sea

CAUCASUS

ARMENIA

ASSYRIA

Anti-Taurus Mountains

GALATIA

CILICIA
Tarsus

Acts 13–15

CYPRUS

Paphos

Antioch

Galatians

SYRIA
Sidon

Matthew   Acts 1–12*
Mark   James
Luke   Jude
John*

ISRAEL
Jerusalem

EDOM
Obadiah

EGYPT

Nile River

Thebes

THE WILDERNESS

Genesis   Numbers
Exodus   Deuteronomy
Leviticus

Red Sea

Caspian Sea

PERSIA
Esther

Zagros Mountains

Susa

River Tigris

Nineveh

MESOPOTAMIA

River Euphrates

Babylon

Ezekiel
Daniel

Joshua   Psalms   Amos
Judges   Ecclesiastes Jonah
Ruth   Proverbs   Micah
1 Samuel   Song of Solomon Nahum
2 Samuel   Isaiah   Habakkuk
1 Chronicles Jeremiah Zephaniah
2 Chronicles Lamentations Haggai
Ezra   Hosea   Zechariah
Nehemiah   Joel   Malachi

ARABIA

* The Book of John was probably begun in Israel and completed at Patmos.
* Acts 13–28 written during Paul's missionary journeys.
* Hebrews authorship and place of origin is uncertain.
* Job authorship and origin is unknown.

6

Books of the Bible

We may be used to thinking of the Bible as one large volume, but it is actually a collection of 66 individual books—39 in the Old Testament and 27 in the New Testament. Some of these books are short; others are longer. There are many different authors and many different styles—from the poetry of the book of Psalms to the more prosaic sermons of Deuteronomy or the narratives of Kings. There are lists of wise sayings, personal letters, and comprehensive inventories of people or items. Some were written in the time of the Roman Empire, while others were begun nearly 3500 years ago!

THE BOOKS OF THE OLD TESTAMENT

Christians traditionally divide the books of the Old Testament into four groupings:

- **The Law** (*Genesis to Deuteronomy*)
- **History** (*Joshua to Esther*)
- **Wisdom** (*Job to the Song of Solomon*)
- **Prophets** (*Isaiah to Malachi*)

THE BOOKS OF THE NEW TESTAMENT

The New Testament can be divided into five sections:

- **Gospels** (*Matthew to John*)
- **History** (*the book of Acts*)
- **Pauline Epistles** (*Romans to Philemon*)
- **General Epistles** (*Hebrews to Jude*)
- **Prophecy** (*the book of Revelation*)

TRANSLATING GOD'S WORD

The earliest translation of the Old Testament was from Hebrew manuscripts into Greek by a group of Jewish monks in the third century BC. In the fourth century AD, the entire Bible was translated into Latin by Jerome, the leading biblical scholar of the time. This definitive version was known as the Vulgate.

The first English versions were translated by John Wycliffe in the late fourteenth century, and later by William Tyndale—who was executed at the stake for his pains in 1536! Nevertheless, Tyndale's work was instrumental in the creation of the definitive King James Bible (also known as the Authorized Version), which aimed to take the best from all earlier translations.

During the nineteenth century, the Bible, or sections of it, were published in some 400 new languages, a number that doubled in the twentieth century.

According to the Wycliffe Global Alliance, by September 2016 the full Bible had been translated into 636 languages, the New Testament into 1442 languages, and stories from the Bible into 1145 other languages, spreading the gospel to every corner of the world!

Many of the words of wisdom set down in the book of Proverbs are attributed to King Solomon.

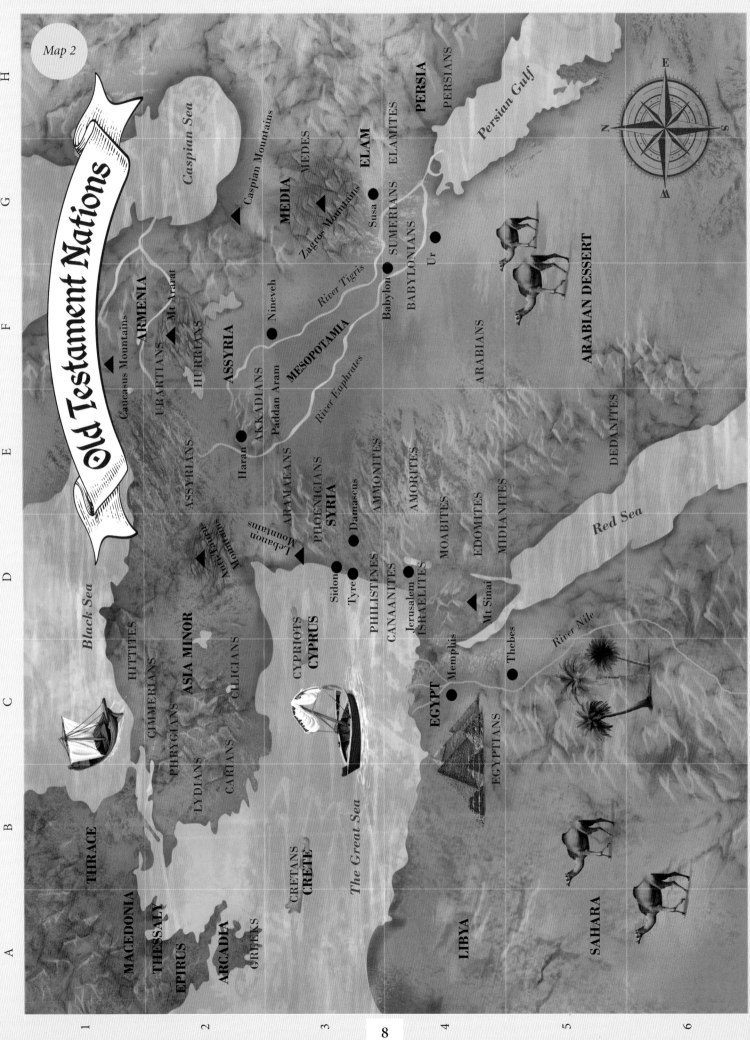

Map 2

Old Testament Nations

Old Testament Nations

ISRAEL

Map 2
D4

Israel as a nation did not exist as we know it during the Old Testament—it was made up of twelve tribes, descended from the sons of Jacob. These tribes, known as the United Monarchy when they were ruled by Saul, David, and Solomon, later split into two main groups, the kingdom of Judah in the south (including the city of Jerusalem) made up of the descendants of Judah and Benjamin, and the kingdom of Israel in the north. Though "Israelites," "Hebrews," and "Jews" tend to be used interchangeably, the Jews actually descended from the kingdom of Judah in the south. After the conquest of Israel by the Assyrians, the northern tribes were dispersed. Judah also fell to invading forces, which resulted in the exile of the Jewish people.

BABYLONIA

Map 2
F4-G4

Babylon is described as a magnificent city with lavish gardens, canals, and impressive walls. On multiple occasions, the Babylonians (often referred to as Chaldeans) took a number of Jews captive, leading to the period in Jewish history known as the Babylonian exile. Perhaps their most notable king was Nebuchadnezzar, who had Daniel as one of his trusted advisors, and who fought against Tyre and Egypt, and captured the city of Jerusalem. In 539 BC Babylon fell to the Persian king Cyrus II, who liberated the exiled Jews, allowing them to return to Jerusalem. The city was later destroyed by Xerxes I of Persia.

PHILISTIA

Map 2
D3

Philistia, a state made up of five main cities (Gaza, Ashdod, Ashkelon, Gath, and Ekron) was the land of the Philistines, who are largely shown in the Bible as the enemy of Israel. Goliath, the giant warrior who was slain by David, was from the city of Gath. His defeat leads to the victory of Saul and the Israelites over the Philistines in the book of 1 Samuel.

SYRIA

Syria, also known as Aram, was a nation that was, for large periods of time, under the control of Assyria. Its capital city, Damascus, was also captured by David (of Israel), although it regained its independence soon after. The destruction of the city was predicted by Isaiah, and indeed it fell to the Assyrians in 732 BC, marking the end of this period of Aramaic Syria.

MEDIA

Media, the land of the Medes, was one of the major powers in its region. It was first controlled by Assyria, then Babylonia, and finally brought into the Persian empire by Cyrus the Great, although the people later rebelled against Darius I and II.

EGYPT

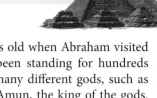

Egypt was already a thousand years old when Abraham visited the land, and the pyramids had been standing for hundreds of years. The people worshipped many different gods, such as Osiris, the ruler of the dead, and Amun, the king of the gods. The ruler of Egypt, known as the Pharaoh, was sometimes considered a god. Joseph, Abraham's great-grandson, was taken to Egypt as a slave but rose to great prominence. His family was welcomed in Egypt, but as they multiplied, they were enslaved until Moses led them out.

ASSYRIA

Assyria, located to the northeast of Israel, was a warlike nation and one of the major powers of antiquity, conquering states and forcing them into allegiance to Assyria and her deities (those of the ancient Mesopotamian religion, with a focus on their national god Ashur). At times, the Assyrians were in control of both Israel and Judah, and were in conflict with the Babylonians. Jonah was sent to Nineveh, the capital of Assyria, to warn them about a coming Babylonian invasion, leading the Assyrians to fast and repent, and consequently God spared their lives. Ultimately, however, the Assyrian empire did fall to Babylon, following the capture of Nineveh in 612 BC.

PERSIA

One of the great nations of antiquity, the Persian people originally migrated from central Asia to the region east of the Persian Gulf. When King Cyrus II, widely known as Cyrus the Great, overthrew Media and conquered Babylon, it marked the beginning of the Persian Achaemenid Empire, which at its height stretched over three continents and 25 nations. Persia was at times sympathetic towards the Jews—King Darius I enabled the completion of the rebuilding of Jerusalem's temple and city walls, and King Xerxes I saved many exiled Jews from persecution. The empire was eventually defeated by Alexander the Great in 331 BC.

EDOM

The Edomites, descendants of Esau, inhabited the region south of the Dead Sea. Throughout its history the nation was in conflict with Israel. The Edomites refused to allow the Israelites to pass through their land on their exodus, and they participated in the plundering of Jerusalem when the city fell to Nebuchadnezzar.

MIDIAN

The Midianites were the descendants of Midian (a son of Abraham) who settled in the deserts of Moab and Edom. An enemy of Israel, they resisted the Israelites as they traveled to Canaan.

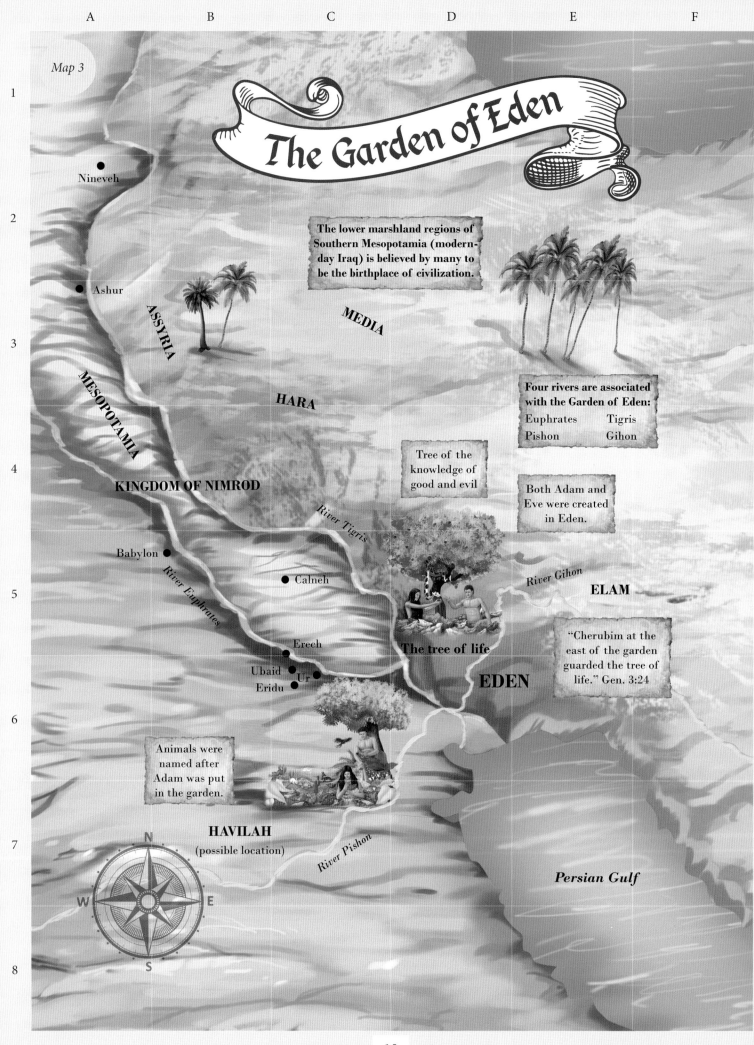

The Garden of Eden

Map 3

The lower marshland regions of Southern Mesopotamia (modern-day Iraq) is believed by many to be the birthplace of civilization.

Four rivers are associated with the Garden of Eden:
Euphrates   Tigris
Pishon   Gihon

Tree of the knowledge of good and evil

Both Adam and Eve were created in Eden.

"Cherubim at the east of the garden guarded the tree of life." Gen. 3:24

The tree of life

Animals were named after Adam was put in the garden.

Nineveh

Ashur

ASSYRIA

MESOPOTAMIA

MEDIA

HARA

KINGDOM OF NIMROD

Babylon

River Euphrates

River Tigris

River Gihon

ELAM

Calneh

Erech

Ubaid   Ur

Eridu

EDEN

HAVILAH
(possible location)

River Pishon

Persian Gulf

N
W   E
S

10

In the Beginning

In the beginning, there was nothing at all. Then God created the heaven and the earth, and illuminated the world with light, making day and night. He separated the water from the land and filled it with beautiful plants and trees, lighting up the sky with the sun, the moon, and the stars. Next he created animals, filling the seas with fish and the land with all kinds of wonderful creatures.

Last of all, God made man and told him to take care of all of his amazing creations. He was pleased with what he had done, and he made the seventh day a day of rest.

Genesis 1-2

Map 3

THE GARDEN OF EDEN

As a home for Adam, the first man, God created the Garden of Eden—a paradise filled with flowers and trees and wonderful animals. He made Eve to be a companion for Adam and told them they could eat from any plant in the garden except one—the tree of the knowledge of good and evil.

But one day the cunning snake tempted Eve to take a bite of the fruit from the tree. She convinced Adam to try some too, and they both ate it. Immediately, it was as if their eyes had been opened, and they covered themselves with fig leaves.

God knew exactly what had happened. To prevent them from eating from the tree of life, he banished them from the Garden of Eden, casting them out into the wide world and placing an angel to guard the entrance.

Genesis 2-3

CAIN AND ABEL

Time passed, and Adam and Eve had two sons, Cain and Abel. One day they each brought offerings to God, Abel pleasing him with the best and fattest of his lambs. However, God wasn't so pleased with Cain's offering of crops.

Cain was very jealous of his brother and furious at both him and God! With evil in his heart, he took Abel out into the fields and murdered him. Of course, God knew what had happened and was very angry. He punished Cain and sent him away to wander from place to place without a home.

Genesis 4

11

Noah and the Flood

STORIES ABOUT THE FLOOD

The story of a great flood being sent to destroy civilization appears in many different cultures from around the world. It is found in the Greek myth of Deucalion, in Hindu texts from India, in the story of the Norse frost giant Bergelmir, and in many more, even stretching to America and Australia!

NOAH BUILDS THE ARK

Many years passed, and soon the world was filled with people. But they were becoming more and more wicked, and it was making God very sad. Finally, he decided to send a flood to clean the world of their sin.

But there was still one good man on earth, whose name was Noah. God told Noah to build an enormous boat so that he and his family might be saved, along with the creatures God had made. Though everyone else made fun of Noah for building a boat in the middle of the land, he trusted God and built the ark.

Genesis 6

Map 4

LONG LIVED

Noah was the grandson of Methuselah, the oldest person in the Bible, who died at 969 years old in the year of the flood. Noah himself was already 500 years old when he became a father, and he died at the age of 950!

Men lived longer the closer in descent they were to Adam and Eve, who had been created to live forever before they disobeyed and were punished by becoming subject to death. The patriarchs (excluding Enoch) who lived before the flood lived an average of 912 years.

THE BUILDING OF THE ARK

God told Noah exactly how to build the ark:

"Build a boat out of good timber, with rooms inside, and cover it with tar inside and out. Make it 450 feet long, 75 feet wide, and 45 feet high. Make a roof for it and leave a space of 18 inches between the roof and the sides. Build it three decks high and put a door in the side."

TWO BY TWO

When the ark was finished, Noah loaded it with food for his family and the animals, and then God sent the animals to the ark, two by two, one male and one female of every kind of animal and bird that lived upon the earth or flew in the skies.

Genesis 7

THE FLOOD

Once they were all safely in, it started to rain. It rained for 40 days and 40 nights, until the earth was completely covered with water. Everything and everyone not on the ark were washed away by the flood.

At last, the rain stopped, and eventually, after 150 days, Noah sent out a dove to see if they could disembark. The dove came back with an olive leaf in its beak, showing that the trees were growing again and that they could all return to the land and start again.

Genesis 7-9

Mount Ararat, in the east of Turkey, is traditionally seen as the resting place of Noah's ark. Even as recently as 2010, Christian explorers claim to have found wood from the ark buried beneath the snow and volcanic debris there.

GOD'S COVENANT WITH NOAH

Noah was filled with gratitude that he had survived, and he made a sacrifice to God. Then God blessed Noah and his family, saying "Be fruitful and multiply." He laid down some rules to help men not to become so wicked, and he made a promise that he would never again send such a dreadful flood. He put a beautiful rainbow in the sky to remind him of this promise.

Genesis 9

Map 4
F1

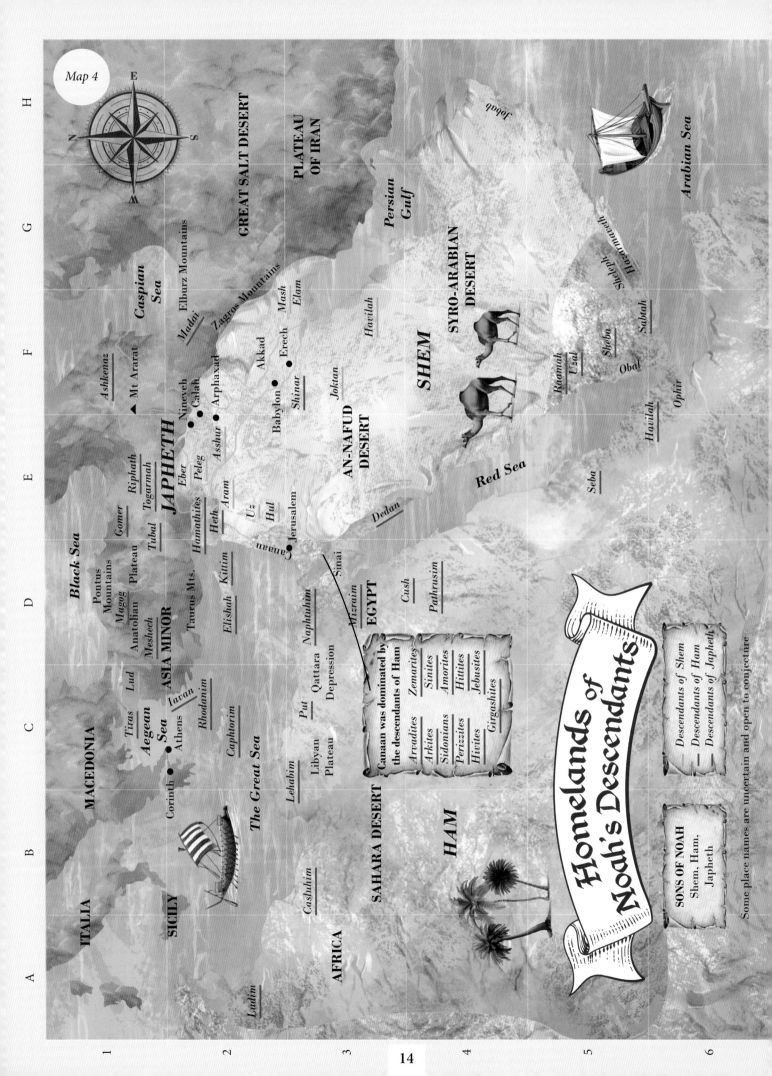

Map 4

N E S W

ITALIA

MACEDONIA

Black Sea

SICILY

Aegean Sea

Corinth ● ● Athens

The Great Sea

AFRICA

SAHARA DESERT

HAM

Tiras
Lud
Ivavan
Rhodanim
Caphtorim

Pontus Mountains
Magog
Anatolian Plateau
Meshech
Taurus Mts.

Gomer
Tubal
Togarmah
Riphath

JAPHETH

Elishah
Kittim

Hamathites
Heth
Aram

Uz
Hul
Jerusalem

Canaan

Sinai

Mizraim

EGYPT

Cush

Pathrusim

Naphtuhim

Qattara Depression

Put

Libyan Plateau

Lehabim

Casluhim

Ludim

Ashkenaz

▲ Mt Ararat

Nineveh ● ● Calah
Asshur ●

Eber
Peleg
Arphaxad

Akkad

Babylon ● ● Erech
Shinar

Mash
Elam

Joktan

Havilah

AN-NAFUD DESERT

Madai
Zagros Mountains

Elburz Mountains

Caspian Sea

GREAT SALT DESERT

PLATEAU OF IRAN

Persian Gulf

SYRO-ARABIAN DESERT

SHEM

Red Sea

Seba

Dedan

Jobab

Shelepth
Hazarmaveth

Sabtah

Sheba

Obal

Raamah
Uzal

Havilah

Ophir

Arabian Sea

Canaan was dominated by the descendants of Ham

Arvadies
Arkites
Sidonians
Perizzites
Hivites

Zemarites
Sinites
Amorites
Hittites
Jebusites
Girgashites

Homelands of Noah's Descendants

Descendants of Shem
Descendants of Ham
Descendants of Japheth

SONS OF NOAH
Shem, Ham, Japheth

Some place names are uncertain and open to conjecture

14

GOD CALLS ABRAHAM

Abraham was a good man who trusted in God. God asked Abraham to leave his home in Ur, his country, and his family and go to another land. He promised to bless him and to make him the father of a great nation.

Abraham had a good home with large flocks of sheep and cattle, but when God told him to leave, he did. He took his wife, Sarah, his nephew, Lot, and his servants and set out for Canaan.

Along the way, God appeared to Abraham and told him, "I will give this land to your children." Sarah and Abraham had been unable to have children, but Abraham was overjoyed at this news and built an altar to God and praised him.

Later, Abraham took his family to Egypt, for there was a terrible famine. By the time he left Egypt to return to Canaan, he had become very wealthy and owned many animals.

Genesis 12-13

Map 5
G4, A4-5,
C4

LOT LEAVES

Abraham and his nephew Lot had flocks of cattle, sheep, and donkeys—so many that there wasn't enough grazing land for them all, and their herdsmen began to fight. Abraham decided that they would have to split up. He gave Lot the first choice of where to go, and Lot chose to leave Canaan and set off east to the green and fertile Jordan Valley. Abraham stayed in Canaan.

After Lot had left, God called Abraham to him. "Look as far as you can. All the land that you can see, I will give to you and to your children forever, and your children shall be like the dust of the earth—for there will be so many of them that no one will be able to count them!"

Genesis 13-14

Map 5
C4, E5

GOD'S PROMISE

Abraham and his wife were very old and hadn't had a child, but Abraham wasn't worried—he trusted God. God told him that he would be a father and that he would have too many descendants to count—as many as the stars in the sky!—and that all this land would belong to them. Then God told him to prepare a sacrifice.

That evening, God spoke to him again, telling him that his descendants would be slaves in a country not their own for 400 years, but that they would at last be free and would return to their own land, and that those who had enslaved them would be punished.

When the sun had set and darkness had fallen, a smoking firepot with a blazing torch appeared and passed between the pieces of the sacrifice as a sign to Abraham from God.

Genesis 15-17

THE FERTILE CRESCENT

The Fertile Crescent (also known as the Cradle of Civilization) is where some of the earliest human civilizations began. This region centered around the Tigris and Euphrates rivers and contained moist and fertile land in an otherise arid and semi-arid part of the world.

The region saw the development of some of the earliest human civilizations, which flourished thanks to the water supplies and agricultural resources available in the Fertile Crescent. It is regarded as the birthplace of agriculture, urbanization, writing, trade, science, history and organized religion.

THE CITY OF UR

Ur was a wealthy port city in the region of Sumer, southern Mesopotamia, in what is modern-day Iraq. The city developed during the reign of the Sumerian kings and had been a major city for hundreds of years when Abraham was born.

According to the Bible, Abraham was from the city of Ur. However, scholars have contested whether Abraham's home was in Ur in Sumer or further north in Mesopotamia in a place called Ura, near the city of Haran.

Map 5
G4, D1

ABRAHAM ENTERTAINS ANGELS

Abraham saw three strangers passing by. He hurried out to meet them, bringing his choicest meat, bread that Sarah had baked for the men to eat, and milk for them to drink.

Then one of the men asked Abraham where his wife was. When Abraham replied that she was inside the tent, the man, who was actually God, told him that within a year Sarah would have given birth to a son. Sarah was listening in the tent and could not help laughing out loud—she was far too old to have children! But God asked, "Why is Sarah laughing? Nothing is too hard for the Lord," and sure enough, nine months later she gave birth to a baby boy named Isaac.

The name Isaac comes from the Hebrew term Yishaq, *meaning "He laughs" or "He will laugh," because Sarah had laughed.*

Over the course of his journey from Ur to Canaan and then later to Egypt, Abraham would have traveled more than 1000 miles.

Genesis 18

Map 5

Abraham's Wanderings

MEDIA

ASSYRIA

MESOPOTAMIA

MITANNI

HITTITE EMPIRE

BABYLONIA (Sumer)

ARABIA

Persian Gulf

Alternative route to Haran

Alternative location of Ur of the Chaldeans

Traditional location of Ur of the Chaldeans

River Tigris

River Euphrates

Abraham's journey from Ur to Canaan

Nineveh

Assur

Babylon

Ur

Haran

Paddan-aram

Mari

Carchemish

Ebla

Hamath

Kadesh

Damascus

Hazor

Shechem

Bethel

Jerusalem

Hebron

Beer-sheba

Kadesh-barnea

CANAAN

Ugarit

Sidon

Tyre

Joppa

Ashkelon

Gaza

Negeb

Midian

Sinai

Egypt

Memphis

River Nile

CYPRUS

The Great Sea

Red Sea

Route of Abraham's rescue of Lot
Abraham's wanderings in the "south country"

Abraham's Wanderings in the Land of Canaan

Damascus

Dan

Lake Chinnereth

Karnaim

Ashtaroth

Ham

River Jordan & Valley

Shechem

Ai

Bethel

Salem (Mt Moriah)

Kiriathaim

Hebron

Dead Sea

Gerar

Beer-sheba

Hormah

Azazon-tamar

Zoar

Kadesh-barnea

Wilderness of Paran

1 2 3 4 5 6

17

ISAAC IS BORN

When Sarah was 90 years old, she gave birth to a baby boy, Isaac, just as God had promised. Abraham and Sarah were overjoyed, but Sarah believed her maidservant Hagar was making fun of her. She was so angry with her that she made Abraham send her away, along with her son, Ishmael, who was also Abraham's son.

Abraham was sad, but God told him things would work out for Ishmael, so he handed Hagar some food and water and sent her and Ishmael into the desert.

Soon all the water was gone, and they began to weep in despair. But an angel spoke to Hagar: "Don't be afraid. God has heard the boy crying. Lift him up and take him by the hand, for he will be the father of a great nation." Then God opened her eyes, and she saw a well of water!

God was with the boy as he grew up. Ishmael lived in the desert and became an archer.

Genesis 21

Map 6
A6

ABRAHAM IS TESTED

Isaac grew up to be a fine young boy, and his father and mother were very proud of him and thankful to God. But one day, God decided to test Abraham's faith. He told Abraham that he must offer the boy as a sacrifice!

Abraham was heartbroken, but his faith in God was absolute, and so he prepared everything just as he had been commanded. He traveled to Mount Moriah and prepared for the sacrifice. But as he lifted up his knife, suddenly an angel spoke to him: "Abraham, Abraham! Don't harm the boy! I know now that you love the Lord your God with all your heart, for you would be willing to give up your own son."

God sent a ram to be sacrificed in the boy's place, and the angel told Abraham that God would truly bless him and his descendants because of his faith.

Genesis 22

Map 6
A5

A WIFE FOR ISAAC

When Isaac had grown into an adult, Abraham asked his most trusted servant to go back to his homeland and find a wife there for his son. When the servant reached his master's hometown, he prayed to God to send him a sign: "Let it be whoever comes to offer water not just to me, but to my camels also."

Before he had finished praying, beautiful Rebekah came out to draw water from the well. When the servant asked her if he might have a drink, she offered him her jar and then hurried to draw water for his camels too. The servant thanked God for listening to his prayers. He explained his mission to Rebekah, and when her father was asked, it was agreed that she should become Isaac's wife. When she traveled back to Canaan to meet her new husband, Isaac fell in love with her instantly, and she with him!

Genesis 24

Map 6
C1

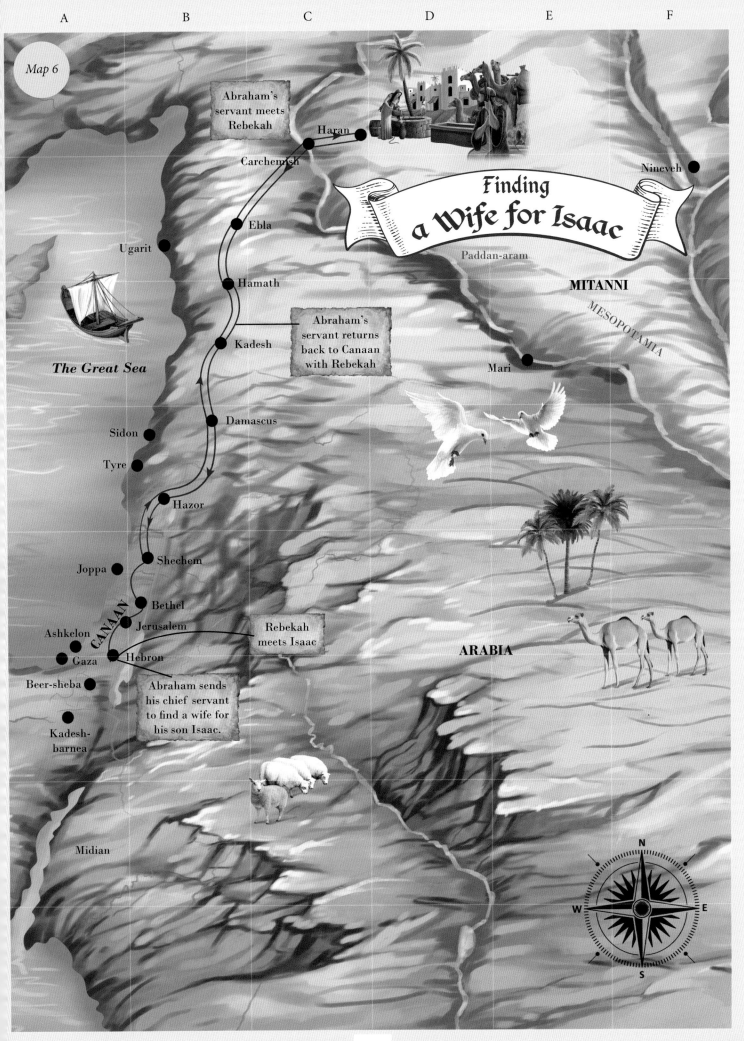

Map 6

A B C D E F

Abraham's servant meets Rebekah

Haran

Carchemish

Nineveh

Finding a Wife for Isaac

Ebla

Ugarit

Paddan-aram

Hamath

MITANNI

MESOPOTAMIA

Abraham's servant returns back to Canaan with Rebekah

Kadesh

Mari

The Great Sea

Damascus

Sidon

Tyre

Hazor

Joppa

Shechem

Bethel

CANAAN

Jerusalem

Rebekah meets Isaac

ARABIA

Ashkelon

Gaza

Hebron

Beer-sheba

Abraham sends his chief servant to find a wife for his son Isaac.

Kadesh-barnea

Midian

N W E S

THE BOWL OF STEW

Rebekah was old before she became pregnant, and when she did, it was with twins. They kicked and pushed so much inside her that she was worried, but God told her that the two boys would one day be the fathers of two nations. The firstborn was a hairy boy, whom they named Esau, and his brother was called Jacob. When they grew up, Esau became a great hunter, while Jacob was quieter and spent more time at home. Isaac loved Esau, but Rebekah was especially fond of Jacob.

One day, Jacob was preparing a stew when his brother came in, ravenous after a long day. When he asked for some of the stew, Jacob told him that he could only have it in exchange for his birthright as the firstborn son. Esau was so hungry and impatient that he agreed!

Genesis 25

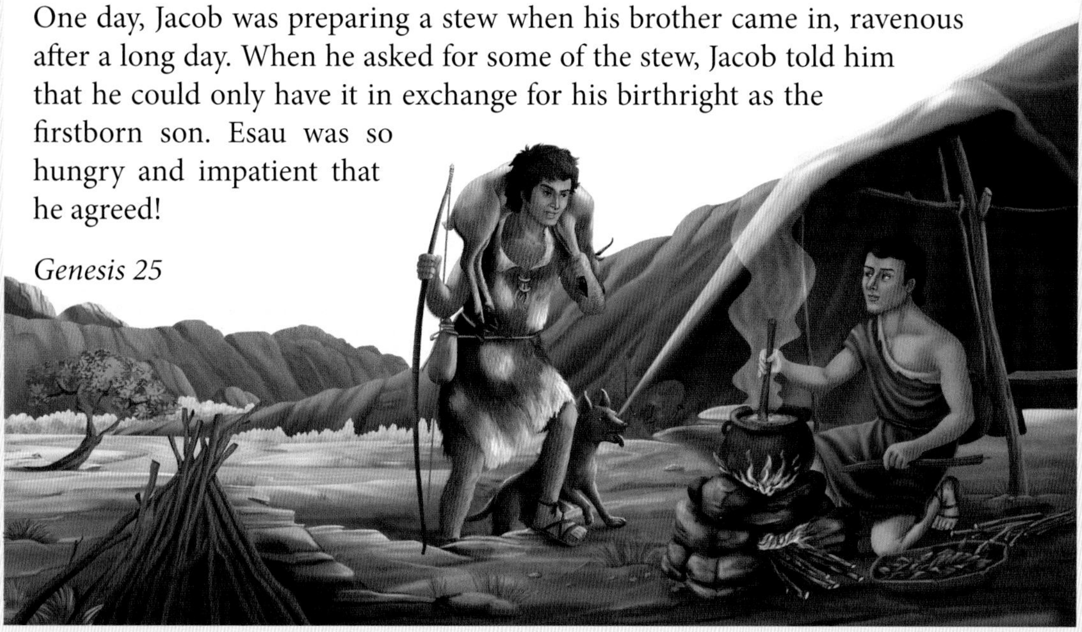

HARAN

The city of Haran, to which Jacob traveled, is located in Padan-aram, in the area generally identified as the upper Mesopotamian region. Mesopotamia is the Greek word for the Hebrew "Aram Naharaim," which means "Aram of the two rivers" (Euphrates and Tigris).

It is situated in the fertile Haran Plain, which is watered by the Balikh River, a major tributary of the Euphrates River. The walls of Haran were 2.5 miles long and had six different gates. Today, only the ruins of the city remain standing.

*Map 7
E1*

DISGUISE

In later years, Jacob cheated Esau out of his father's blessing too. When Isaac was very old and nearly blind, he wished to give his blessing to his eldest son. He told Esau to go off and kill an animal and prepare it for him to eat, and then he would bless him.

But Rebekah overheard their conversation and was determined that her favorite son, Jacob, would receive the blessing. She told Jacob to fetch two young goats, which she prepared for Isaac. Then, with the help of his mother, Jacob disguised himself as Esau. He wore goatskins around his arms so that he would be hairy like his brother, and then took in the food.

Jacob didn't sound like his brother, but he felt like him, and so Isaac gave him his blessing to be in charge of the family when he died.

When Esau found out what had happened, he was so angry that he wanted to kill his younger brother! Rebekah knew that Jacob must leave home immediately, so she sent him to the house of his uncle who lived in Haran to keep him safe.

Genesis 27

Map 7

Jacob Travels to Haran

ASSYRIA

River Tigris

River Euphrates

Nineveh

Babylon

ARABIA

Jacob served in Laban's house for 20 years before fleeing back to Canaan

Jacob worked for Laban, married Rachel and Leah

PADDAN-ARAM

Mari

Jacob set out in haste from Beer-sheba and camped at Bethel (formerly Luz) before continuing onto Paddan-aram

Laban caught up with Jacob in the hill country of Gilead. Then Jacob traveled on and wrestled with God at Peniel

Jacob dreamed of a stairway to heaven

Esau came up from Seir and met Jacob in peace; Jacob then continued on as far as Shechem

Haran

Carchemish

Ebla

Hamath

Kadesh

Damascus

Hazor

Succoth

Peniel

Sidon

Tyre

Shechem

Joppa

Salem

GILEAD

Bethel

Hebron

Beer-sheba

Mount Seir

CANAAN

Ashkelon

Gaza

Kadesh-barnea

CYPRUS

The Great Sea

Jacob built an altar at Shechem

Negeb

SINAI

MIDIAN

EGYPT

River Nile

Memphis

21

JACOB'S DREAM

Jacob set off to travel to Haran, to the house of his uncle Laban. On the way he stopped for the night. Using a hard stone as a pillow, he lay down to sleep. That night he had a dream. He saw a stairway resting on the earth,

with its top reaching to heaven, and angels were walking up and down it.

At the very top stood the Lord, and he said, "I am the Lord, the God of your father Abraham and the God of Isaac. I will give you and your descendants the land on which you lie. Your descendants will be like the dust of the earth, and you will spread to the west and the east, to the north and the south. I am with you and will watch over you wherever you go, and I will bring you back to this land. I won't leave you until I have done what I have promised!"

Genesis 28

Map 7
E1

TRICKED INTO MARRIAGE

Jacob worked in the house of his uncle Laban, and he fell in love with Laban's younger daughter, Rachel. His uncle agreed that if he worked for him for seven years, he could then marry Rachel. However, when, after seven years, the marriage took place, and Jacob lifted the veil from his wife's face, it was not Rachel standing before him, but her elder sister, Leah! He had been tricked!

Laban told him that it was the custom that the oldest daughter marry first, but he said that if Jacob would promise to work for him for another seven years, then he could marry his beloved Rachel. Jacob loved her so much that he agreed.

Rachel was always his favorite wife, but God took pity on Leah and blessed her with four strong sons, while it was many years before Rachel had a son.

Genesis 29

PARTING WAYS

Although Jacob felt it was time to return home, his uncle wanted him to stay. Laban agreed to give him, as his wages, all the marked or speckled animals in the herds, but then he tried to cheat Jacob by rounding up any marked animals and sending them away with his sons so that all the new animals would be born without marks!

But God told Jacob to place some freshly peeled branches in the animals' water troughs when the strong, healthy animals came to drink, and all the new animals that were born to them were marked or speckled. In this way all the strong animals went to Jacob and all the weak animals went to Laban.

Jacob knew that his uncle would continue to cheat him, so one day he set off for home, along with all his family, servants, and animals. Laban chased after him, but in the end he let him go.

Genesis 30-31

WRESTLING WITH GOD

Jacob was worried as he returned home with his family, for he didn't know how his brother Esau would greet him. When a messenger said that Esau was coming to meet him with 400 men, Jacob feared the worst. He sent some of his servants ahead with gifts for his brother to help make peace. Then he sent his family and everything he owned across the river. Jacob himself stayed behind alone to pray.

Suddenly a man appeared, and the two of them wrestled together until daybreak. When the man saw that he could not overpower him, he touched Jacob's hip so that it was wrenched. He cried out to Jacob to let him go, but Jacob replied, "Not unless you bless me!"

Then the man said, "Your name will no longer be Jacob, but Israel, because you have struggled with God and with men and have overcome."

When Jacob asked his name, he would give no reply. But he blessed Jacob, and Jacob understood that he had wrestled with God himself!

Genesis 32-33

After Jacob is tested, God changes his name to Israel. The name "Israel" comes from two Hebrew words meaning "wrestle" and "God"—referring to Jacob's struggle with God.

Map 7
D4

RETURNING TO BETHEL

Map 7
C4

God spoke to Jacob and told him to go to Bethel. So Jacob traveled with his family and servants to Bethel, where he built an altar to God to thank him for his mercy.

When they left Bethel, Rachel, who was pregnant for the second time, went into labor, but things didn't go smoothly. Before she breathed her last breath, Rachel saw her lovely baby boy and named him Ben-Oni, which means "son of my sorrow," although his father called him Benjamin, "son of my right hand." Jacob was heartbroken and built a pillar over her tomb.

Now Jacob had twelve sons. The sons of Leah were Reuben, Simeon, Levi, Judah, Issachar, and Zebulun. Joseph and Benjamin were the sons of Rachel. Dan and Naphtali were the sons of Rachel's maidservant, and Gad and Asher were the sons of Leah's maidservant.

Genesis 35-36

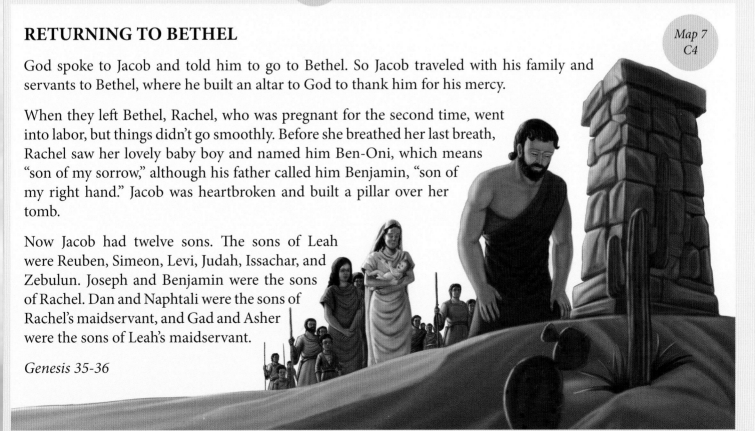

PHARAOH'S DREAMS

One night, Pharaoh had a strange dream. He was standing by the Nile when out of the river came seven cows, healthy and fat, and they grazed among the reeds. After them, seven other cows, ugly and thin, came up out of the Nile and stood beside them. Then the thin cows ate up the fat cows and yet looked just as thin and sickly as before!

Pharaoh had another dream. Seven healthy heads of grain were growing on a single stalk. Then seven more heads of grain sprouted, and these were thin and scorched by the wind. The thin heads of grain swallowed up the seven healthy, full heads.

In the morning, Pharaoh felt worried. He sent for all the magicians and wise men of Egypt, but no one could interpret the dreams.

Genesis 41

WHAT CAN IT MEAN?

Just then the wine bearer remembered Joseph, and the slave was brought before mighty Pharaoh, who asked him to explain his dream. "I cannot do it," Joseph replied, "but God will be able to explain."

Once Pharaoh had told his dream, Joseph replied, "These two dreams are really one and the same. The seven cows and the seven heads of grain are seven years. The land will be blessed with seven years of healthy crops and bumper harvests, but they will be followed by seven years of dreadful famine. You will need to plan carefully to prepare for what lies ahead."

Pharaoh spoke to his advisors and then to Joseph, saying, "Since God has made all this known to you, I will put you in charge of my land. You will be second only to me in all of Egypt." He put his own signet ring on Joseph's finger, placed a gold chain around his neck, and dressed him in fine clothes!

Genesis 41

Map 7
A/B5-6

A WISE LEADER

Joseph was thirty years old when he entered the service of Pharaoh, king of Egypt. Riding in a fine chariot, he traveled throughout the land making sure that food was put aside for the times of hardship ahead of them. Just as he had foretold, the country was blessed with seven years of bumper crops, and so much grain was stored in the cities that he gave up counting it.

After seven years, the famine began. When the people of Egypt began to run out of food, Pharaoh told them to go to Joseph.

Now Joseph opened up the storehouses and sold the corn that had been put away so carefully. No one in Egypt went hungry. In fact, there was so much food in Egypt that people from other countries traveled there to buy food, for the famine was severe throughout the world.

Genesis 41

THE BROTHERS BUY GRAIN

In Canaan, the famine had hit Joseph's family hard too. Jacob decided to send his sons to buy corn in Egypt. Only Benjamin stayed behind, for Jacob could not bear to lose his youngest son. When they reached Egypt, the brothers bowed down before Joseph. With his golden chain and fine clothes, they didn't recognize him, but Joseph could see his dreams becoming reality as they bowed their heads low and begged to buy food.

Joseph wanted to see if his brothers had changed at all, and so he planned to test their honesty and loyalty. He accused them of being spies. The brothers frantically denied it, so he agreed to let them go back to Canaan with corn—but only if they return with their youngest brother.

Jacob didn't want to let Benjamin go, but in the end he had to agree, and so the brothers returned with more money to pay for the grain.

Genesis 42-43

Map 7
A4-5

TREACHERY

Joseph was so overcome when he saw Benjamin that he had to hide his face. He had his servants feed the brothers and then sent them on their way with more corn, but not before hiding a silver cup in Benjamin's sack. The brothers were traveling home when guards came upon them and dragged them back to the palace.

"Thieves!" shouted Joseph. "I treated you with kindness, and you repay me by stealing!"

"There must be some mistake!" cried the brothers, but when the guards checked, there was the silver cup in Benjamin's sack.

The horrified brothers fell to their knees. "My Lord," they cried, "take any one of us, but do not take Benjamin, for his father's heart would break!"

Genesis 44

THE LONG-LOST BROTHER

At this, Joseph knew that his brothers really had changed. They cared so much for their little brother and for how upset their father would be, that any one of them would have given himself up to save Benjamin. Crying tears of joy, Joseph went to hug them, and to their joy and amazement, told them who he really was. He told them not to feel too bad about what had happened, for it had all been part of God's plan. "I was sent to rule in Egypt so that you would not starve in Canaan!" he said.

At first, they could hardly believe that this great and important man was really their long-lost brother, but when they did, they were filled with joy, for they had had many years to feel sorry for what they had done.

Genesis 45

MOVING TO EGYPT

Now it was time to tell Jacob the good news. When the brothers returned saying that his beloved son Joseph was not only alive and well, but governor of all Egypt, Jacob could hardly believe his ears! But when he saw all the fine gifts that Joseph had sent him, he had to believe his eyes!

Jacob gathered up all his belongings, his herds and flocks, and traveled to Egypt with his family. God reassured him, telling him that he would lead them out of Egypt once again when the time was right.

Joseph came to meet his father in a great chariot and led him back to Egypt, where he and his family were well treated and given land near the Canaan border to tend their animals.

Genesis 46-47

Map 7 A/B5-6

THE DEATH OF JACOB

Now Jacob was growing old. Before he died, he called all his sons together to give them each a special blessing, for they were to form the twelve tribes of Israel, and he named Joseph "a prince among his brothers."

He made Joseph promise to bury him in Canaan, in the spot where he had buried his wife Leah, and where Isaac and Rebecca were buried before her, and Abraham and Sarah before them. When Jacob had breathed his last breath, with Pharaoh's permission, all Jacob's family, except the children and those who tended the animals, set off to Canaan, where they buried their father Jacob, also known as Israel.

Genesis 48-50

Map 7 C4-5

PATRIARCHS OF ISRAEL

Map 8

Hagar —————— **Abraham** —— Sarah

Ishmael
(ancestor of the Ishmaelites and patriarch of Qedar)

Isaac —— Rebecca

Jacob
(father of Israel)

Esau
(father of the Edomites)

Zilpah
(Leah's handmaid)

Leah
(older sister)

Rachel
(younger sister)

Bilhah
(Rachel's handmaid)

THE TWELVE TRIBES OF ISRAEL

Gad *("Good fortune")*
Asher *("Happy")*

Reuben *("See, a son")*
Simeon *("He who hears")*
Levi *("Attached")*
Judah *("Praise")*
Issachar *("Hired")*
Zebulun *("Honored")*

Joseph *("May he add")*
Benjamin
("Son of my right hand")

Dan *("He has vindicated")*
Naphtali *("My struggle")*

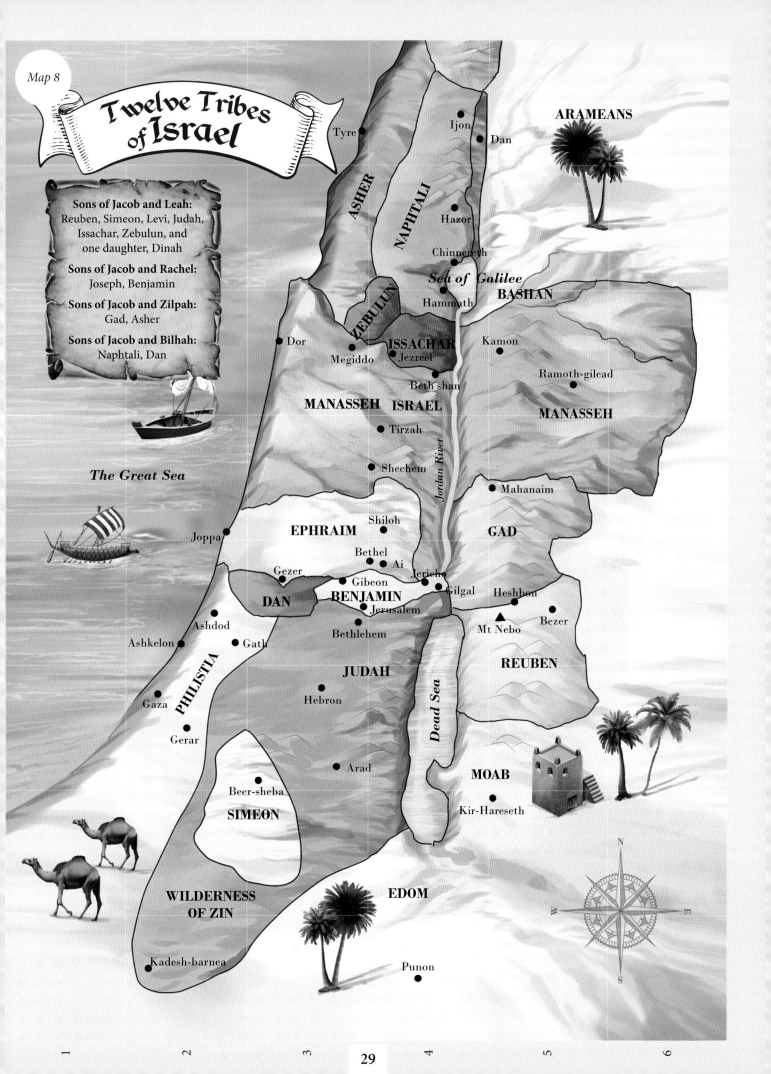

Map 8

Twelve Tribes of Israel

Sons of Jacob and Leah:
Reuben, Simeon, Levi, Judah, Issachar, Zebulun, and one daughter, Dinah

Sons of Jacob and Rachel:
Joseph, Benjamin

Sons of Jacob and Zilpah:
Gad, Asher

Sons of Jacob and Bilhah:
Naphtali, Dan

ARAMEANS

Tyre

Ijon

Dan

ASHER

NAPHTALI

Hazor

Chinnereth

Sea of Galilee

BASHAN

Hammath

ZEBULUN

ISSACHAR

Kamon

Dor

Megiddo

Jezreel

Ramoth-gilead

Beth shan

MANASSEH   ISRAEL

MANASSEH

Tirzah

The Great Sea

Shechem

Jordan River

Mahanaim

Shiloh

EPHRAIM

GAD

Joppa

Bethel

Ai

Gezer

Jericho

Gibeon

Gilgal

Heshbon

DAN   BENJAMIN

Jerusalem

Bezer

Ashdod

Bethlehem

Mt Nebo

Ashkelon

Gath

REUBEN

Gaza

PHILISTIA

JUDAH

Gerar

Hebron

Arad

MOAB

Beer-sheba

Kir-Hareseth

SIMEON

Dead Sea

WILDERNESS OF ZIN

EDOM

Kadesh-barnea

Punon

N
W   E
S

Moses and the Exodus

THE HEBREWS BECOME SLAVES

The years passed. Joseph and his brothers were long dead, but their families continued to grow, and by now there were many, many Hebrews in Egypt. The new king believed that there were too many of them in his country, and he feared that they would become too strong, so the Egyptians put guards over the Hebrews and turned them into slaves. They forced them to work the land and build for them.

The Hebrews were badly treated, yet still their numbers grew, for the women were blessed by God. Now the new king ordered that any girls born to the Hebrews could live, but any boys must be killed. When the Hebrew midwives failed to do as he asked, he ordered that all baby boys must be drowned in the river Nile!

Exodus 1

Map 9

BABY IN THE REEDS

Moses was a Hebrew baby boy. His mother knew that if the king found out about him, he would be killed, so she made a basket for him out of bulrushes and lowered him into the water among the reeds.

After a while, the king's daughter came down to the river. She heard a strange noise and pulled back the reeds to see a baby boy. She picked him up and held him. "This must be one of the Hebrew babies," she said softly.

Moses' sister, Miriam, was secretly watching from nearby. She bravely stepped forward and offered to find someone to nurse the baby. When the princess agreed, Miriam fetched her own mother, and so it was that Miriam's mother looked after her own son until he was old enough for the princess to take him to the palace.

Exodus 2

THE BURNING BUSH

When Moses grew up, he was shocked to see how the Egyptians treated his fellow Hebrews. One day he lost his temper and killed an Egyptian who was brutally beating a Hebrew slave. He fled the country, traveled to Midian, and became a shepherd.

One day, while Moses was tending his sheep, he noticed that a nearby bush was on fire, yet the leaves of the bush were not burning! As he stepped closer, he heard God's voice say, "Take off your sandals, Moses, for this is holy ground. I am the God of your father, the God of Abraham, of Isaac, and of Jacob."

God told Moses that it was time for his people to be freed. He told him to go to Pharaoh and demand their release. Moses was terrified at the thought of speaking to mighty Pharaoh, but God sent him to Egypt and sent his brother, Aaron, to help him.

Exodus 2-4

Map 9 G5

PHARAOH SAYS NO

When Moses and Aaron came before Pharaoh and said, "The God of Israel asks that you let his people go so that they may hold a festival to him in the desert," Pharaoh replied, "Who is this God of Israel? I don't know him, and I won't let the Hebrews go!" He was so angry that he made the slaves work even harder.

So Moses and Aaron went back to Pharaoh, who demanded some proof of their God. Aaron threw down his staff on the ground, and it was instantly transformed into a snake! But the king's magicians huddled together and performed sorcery, and when they threw their staffs on the ground, they too turned into snakes. Even though Aaron's snake swallowed them all up, the king's heart was hardened, and he would not let the Hebrews go.

Exodus 5-7

THE PLAGUES

Then the Lord sent a series of plagues upon the Egyptians. First he changed the waters of the Nile into blood. All the fish died, and the air stank. He sent a plague of frogs to cover the countryside and fill the houses. Next, the dust on the ground was turned into gnats, and after them came a swarm of flies. He sent a plague among the livestock of the land but spared those belonging to the Hebrews. Then the Egyptians were afflicted with horrible boils. But still Pharaoh wouldn't change his mind!

God sent a terrible hailstorm that stripped the land, followed by a swarm of locusts. Nothing green remained in all Egypt! After this, God sent total darkness to cover Egypt for three whole days.

Each time Pharaoh refused to let the Hebrews go, for God had hardened his heart.

But now the time had come for the most dreadful plague of all . . .

Exodus 7-10

Map 9

THE PASSOVER

Moses warned Pharaoh that God would pass through the country at midnight, and every firstborn son in the land would die, from the son of Pharaoh himself, to the son of the lowliest slave girl, and even the firstborn of the animals as well. But Pharaoh would not listen.

Moses told the Israelites what God wanted them to do to be spared. Each household was to kill a lamb, smear some of the blood on the doorframe, and then eat the meat in a special way. That night God passed throughout Egypt, and the next day the land was filled with the sound of mourning, for all the firstborn sons had died—even the son of mighty Pharaoh. But the Hebrews were spared.

Now the Egyptians couldn't get rid of the Hebrews quick enough, and so they prepared to leave.

Genesis 11-12

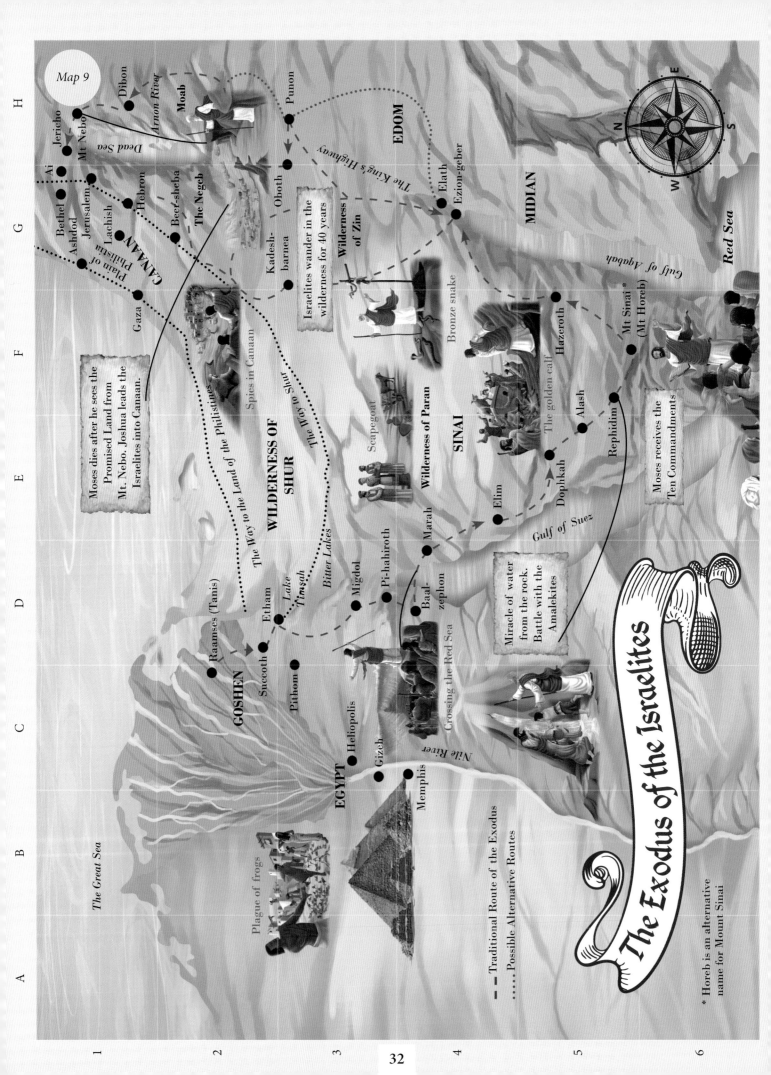

Map 9

The Exodus of the Israelites

The Great Sea

EGYPT
Gizeh
Heliopolis
Memphis
Nile River
Plague of frogs

GOSHEN
Raames (Tanis)
Succoth
Pithom

Etham
Lake Timsah
Bitter Lakes
Migdol
Pi-hahiroth
Baal-zephon
Crossing the Red Sea

WILDERNESS OF SHUR
The Way to Shur
The Way to the Land of the Philistines

CANAAN
Plain of Philistia
Gaza
Ashdod
Lachish
Jerusalem
Bethel
Ai
Jericho
Mt Nebo
Hebron
Beer-sheba
The Negeb
Kadesh-barnea

Dead Sea
Dibon
Arnon River
Moab
Punon
Oboth
The King's Highway

EDOM

Spies in Canaan

Moses dies after he sees the Promised Land from Mt. Nebo. Joshua leads the Israelites into Canaan.

Israelites wander in the wilderness for 40 years

Wilderness of Zin
Elath
Ezion-geber

MIDIAN

Scapegoat
Bronze snake
Wilderness of Paran
SINAI
The golden calf
Hazeroth
Alash
Dophkah
Elim
Marah
Rephidim
Gulf of Suez
Gulf of Aqabah
Mt Sinai*
(Mt Horeb)

Red Sea

Moses receives the Ten Commandments

Miracle of water from the rock. Battle with the Amalekites

- - - Traditional Route of the Exodus
.... Possible Alternative Routes

* Horeb is an alternative name for Mount Sinai

32

Map 9
C2-D3

THE EXODUS

The Hebrews traveled southward across the desert, towards the Red Sea. By day, God sent a great column of cloud to guide them, and by night they followed a pillar of fire. Yet their troubles were far from over, for Pharaoh was regretting his decision to let them go and had set off with his army to bring them back.

All those flying hooves and grinding wheels set off a huge cloud of dust that the Hebrews could see coming from miles away, and they panicked, for now their way was barred by the waters of the Red Sea. "Why did you bring us all this way, just to have us killed or dragged back into slavery?" cried the terrified Hebrews to Moses. "It would have been better for us to serve the Egyptians than to die in the desert!"

Exodus 12-13

CROSSING THE RED SEA

The people wrung their hands in fear as the dust thrown up by the Egyptian army grew nearer and nearer, but Moses trusted God and stood firm. "God will look after us," he said confidently, "and he will crush our enemy."

God told Moses to raise his staff and stretch out his hand over the sea to divide the water so that the Israelites could go through the sea on dry ground. The column of cloud moved between the Hebrews and the Egyptians so that the Egyptians could not see what was happening, and Moses stood before the sea and raised his hand. All that night the Lord drove the sea back with a strong east wind and turned it into dry land. The waters were divided, and the Israelites went through the sea on dry ground, with a wall of water on their right and on their left!

Exodus 14

Map 9
D4

DROWNED

The Egyptians were hard on the heels of the Hebrews and, without hesitation, followed them into the sea, along the path God had made. But God struck them with confusion so that the wheels of the chariots came off and everyone was in chaos. Then he closed the waters together, and the Egyptians were swept under the sea. Of all that mighty army, there were no survivors—not one horse, not one soldier!

The people of Israel, safe on the other shore of the Red Sea, were filled with gratitude and relief, and they sang and danced in their joy. They knew that their God was both mighty and merciful, and they praised him greatly.

Exodus 14-15

FOOD AND WATER IN THE DESERT

Moses led the Israelites into the desert, but very soon they grew hungry and thirsty and became discontented. Once again God helped his people. One evening a flock of quail came into the camp, and the next morning the ground was covered with white flakes that tasted like wafers made with honey. They called this manna.

When they needed water, God told Moses to take his staff and strike a rock, and from the rock flowed good, clear, fresh drinking water.

The people of Israel wandered through the desert for many, many years, and all that time the Lord looked after them and gave them food and water.

Exodus 15-17

Map 9
F5

HANDS UP!

The Israelites came under attack from a tribe of nomads called the Amelikites. Moses told Joshua, his most trusted warrior, to lead his men into battle, while Moses watched from the hill, holding the staff he had been given by God.

The next day, the battle was fierce and terrible. Moses stood at the top of the hill with his brother, Aaron, and a man named Hur. When he held his hands up in the air, his men would start winning the fight, but when he lowered his hands, the battle would swing the other way!

Moses kept his hands held high for as long as he could, but as time passed, his arms grew tired. At last, it seemed he could hold them up no longer. But Aaron and Hur found a large rock for Moses to sit on, and then they each took one of his arms and held it up for him in the air until the sun dropped below the horizon. And so with God's help, Joshua and his men defeated the Amelikites.

Exodus 17

Map 9
F5

THE TEN COMMANDMENTS

Moses led the people to Mount Sinai. There, the Lord spoke to Moses and told him that if the people would honor and obey him, he would always be with them. He gave Moses many laws that would help the Israelites live happily together. The most famous of these are the Ten Commandments.

You shall have no other gods before me.
You shall not make any false idols.
You shall not misuse my name.
Remember the Sabbath and keep it holy.
Honor your father and your mother.
You shall not murder.
You shall not commit adultery.
You shall not steal.
You shall not tell lies.
You shall not envy anything belonging to your neighbour.

These laws encouraged the Israelites to put God first, but also to think about those around them and to treat them with respect and kindness. God gave Moses two stone tablets with the commandments engraved on them.

Exodus 19-20

Map 9
F5

A PLACE TO WORSHIP

God told Moses to build a special place to keep the stone tablets. They were to be kept inside a wooden chest covered with the purest gold, known as the Ark of the Covenant. This was to be kept inside an inner shrine, in a large tent known as the tabernacle, which would travel with the Israelites wherever they went, and so they carried the presence of the Lord with them on their travels through the desert.

Exodus 25-27

THE DAY OF ATONEMENT

God gave Moses special instructions for Aaron. Aaron was to make sacrifices to offer atonement for his own sins and for those of his family and servants. Then he was to take two goats from the people. One was to be sacrificed to God, and the other was to take on all the sins of the Israelites and then to be sent away into the desert. It was a "scapegoat" to carry away the sins of all the people.

This ceremony was to take place each year and was to be known as the Day of Atonement. It was to be a day to be spent in prayer and thought, to seek forgiveness from God. God commanded the people to fast for the duration of the day.

"All this you shall do," said God, "because on this day atonement will be made for you. Then you will be clean from all your sins in my sight."

Leviticus 16

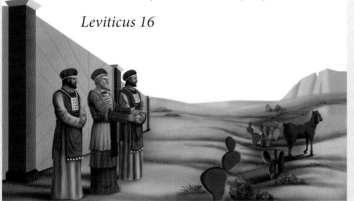

THE GOLDEN CALF

While Moses was up on the mountain, the people began to believe he would never come back down. They asked Aaron to make them gods to lead them. Aaron had them gather their gold jewelry and used it to make a golden calf, which he placed on an altar. The people gathered round and began to worship it.

When Moses came down from the mountain with the tablets and saw the people singing and dancing around the golden calf, he was so furious that he threw the tablets to the ground. Next, he burned the calf and ground it to powder. God punished those who had sinned with a plague.

Exodus 32

Map 9
F5

WATER FROM THE ROCK

The people were constantly complaining, for they were still in the desert and were without water and thirsty. Moses and Aaron asked God to help once more, and he told them to take the staff and gather everyone before a large rock. "Speak to that rock before their eyes, and it will pour out its water," he commanded them.

Moses and Aaron gathered the people. "Listen, you rebels, must we bring you water out of this rock?" Moses said, and then he struck the rock twice with his staff. Water gushed out, and everyone was able to drink.

But God was disappointed because Moses hadn't followed his instructions, nor had he given the credit to God, and so he told the brothers that they would never enter the Promised Land.

Numbers 20

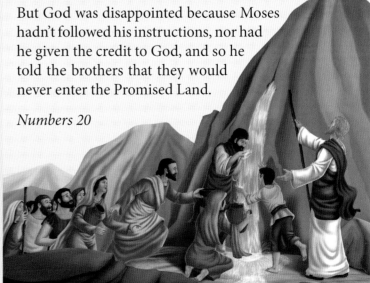

THE BRONZE SNAKE

The Israelites had to travel far in the desert. God helped them to overcome the people and cities that stood in their way, but still the people complained. They spoke against God and against Moses, despite all that had been done for them.

God was fed up with their ingratitude. He sent venomous snakes into their camp, and many Israelites died. The people came to Moses and said, "It was wrong of us to speak against God. Please ask him to take the snakes away!" So Moses prayed.

Then God said to him, "Make a snake and put it up on a pole. Anyone who is bitten can look at it and live." So Moses made a bronze snake and put it up on a pole. When anyone was bitten and looked at the bronze snake, he lived.

Numbers 21

*Map 9
G3*

TIME FOR CHANGE

God told Moses that it would soon be time to leave his people. God said he would let him see the land promised to the Israelites but would not let him enter it. Moses asked God to choose someone to lead the people after his death, and the Lord chose Joshua, who had already shown his faith in God.

Now, the Reubenites and Gadites had very large herds of cattle. They asked if they could stay on the east side of the River Jordan, for the land was good for grazing. Moses agreed that if all their men helped in the fight to conquer Canaan, then after their victory they could claim this land.

God told the Israelites they must drive out the inhabitants of the land before them and destroy all their carved images and idols and temples, for God was not giving the Israelites the land because they were good, but because those who lived there were wicked.

Numbers 27; 32

MOSES SEES THE PROMISED LAND

It was time for Moses to leave his people, but before he went, he gathered them together and said, "You are truly blessed! Who is like you, a people saved by the Lord? He is your shield and helper and your glorious sword. Your enemies will cower before you, and you will trample down their high places."

Moses climbed Mount Nebo, and the Lord showed him the whole land of Canaan in the distance—the plains and the valleys, the cities and the villages, all the way to the sea. Then Moses died. He was a hundred and twenty years old when he passed away, yet his eyes were not weak nor was his strength gone. The people mourned for thirty days. They knew that there would never be another prophet like him, who had spoken with the Lord face to face.

Deuteronomy 33-34

*Map 9
H1*

SPIES!

For many years the Israelites had wandered in the harsh desert, but now it was time to cross the River Jordan into the Promised Land, where food and water were plentiful and the land green and lush. Joshua sent two spies into the city of Jericho, on the far banks of the river. They spent the night in the home of a woman named Rahab, but the king heard there were spies in his city and sent soldiers to search for them. Rahab hid the men on her

roof, and when the soldiers came knocking, she sent them away. Then she gave the spies some rope so they could lower themselves down, for the house was part of the city wall. "The people of Jericho live in fear of your coming," she told them, "for we have heard how powerful your God is. Please spare me and my family when you attack Jericho!"

The spies promised to spare Rahab and her family and told her to tie a red cord to her window as a sign. But they warned her not to speak a word about them, for if she did she would be shown no mercy.

Joshua 1-4

Map 9
H1

CROSSING THE RIVER

The River Jordan was in flood. The swift-flowing waters were treacherous, and there was no bridge or ford. Yet God had told the people that today they would cross into the Promised Land. Joshua sent the priests ahead, carrying the Ark of the Covenant. As soon as their feet touched the water, it stopped flowing and made a huge wall, and a dry path stretched before them. The priests made their way to the middle of the riverbed, and then the people of Israel began to cross safely over. There were so many that it took all day to cross, but by nightfall they had finally arrived in the land promised to them by God for so many years.

Before the priests finished crossing the river, Joshua had one man from each of the twelve tribes of Israel lift a stone from the middle of the riverbed. As soon as the priests stepped onto the shore, the river came crashing down once more. Joshua collected the twelve stones and built them up into a mound as a reminder to the people of all that God had done for them.

Joshua 5

By the time Joshua (whose name in Hebrew means "the Lord is salvation") led the Israelites into the Promised Land, they had spent forty years in the wilderness.

Under his leadership, the Israelites conquered the land of Canaan, and Joshua divided the land among the twelve tribes.

THE WALLS OF JERICHO

When Joshua led the Israelites across the river Jordan and into the Promised Land, the first city they needed to conquer was the high-walled city of Jericho.

God told Joshua exactly what to do. For six days the Israelites marched around the city, and on the seventh day, having marched around the city seven times, the priests blew their trumpets loudly, the people shouted out, and the huge walls of Jericho crumbled and fell before them in a cloud of dust!

The story of how the Lord had helped Joshua spread throughout the land and filled the people of neighboring towns and cities with fear.

Joshua 6

Map 9
H1

CITIES OF REFUGE

These were six Levitical towns in which the perpetrators of manslaughter could claim the right of asylum:

KEDESH
Map 10 G4

The Canaanite royal city of Kedesh was conquered by the Israelites under the leadership of Joshua. Ownership of Kedesh was assigned by lot to the tribe of Naphtali. Subsequently, at the command of God, Kedesh was set apart by Joshua as a Levitical city and one of the cities of refuge.

GOLAN
Map 10 F5

The city of Golan lay in the territory of Manasseh near the Sea of Galilee and was the most northerly of the cities of refuge east of the Jordan.

RAMOTH
Map 10 E5

Ramoth, or Ramoth-Gilead (meaning "Heights of Gilead"), was a Levitical city east of the Jordan river. It was located in the territorial allotment of the tribe of Gad.

SHECHEM
Map 10 E3

Shechem is the location where both Abraham and Jacob built altars to God, and where, after the death of Solomon, the tribes of Israel gathered and decided to split into two separate nations. It became the first capital of the kingdom of Israel.

BEZER
Map 10 D5

Bezer, set apart by Moses for the Reubenites, was one of three cities of refuge on the east of the Jordan.

HEBRON
Map 10 C3

Hebron is venerated by Christians, Jews, and Muslims for its association with Abraham, who lived in Hebron for a long time and was indeed buried there (according to tradition, along with Isaac, Jacob, and their wives). Islam regards it as one of their holiest cities, and it is also one of the four holy cities of Judaism.

LIFE IN THE PROMISED LAND

Map 10

When the Israelites first settled in the Promised Land, fresh from their travels in the desert and the exhortations of Moses, they had the best of intentions and planned to keep their covenant with God. However, as the years passed, they became discontented and forgot about their promises. They fell into evil ways, and God sent them trials and tribulations in the form of enemies, such as the Philistines. Each time, he also sent a hero or heroine to protect his people. This was the time of the Judges, of wise Deborah and strong Samson, and of one of the greatest of all prophets—Samuel. But when Samuel grew old, Israel demanded a king, fearful of the future and no longer wholly trusting in God.

God chose a young man named Saul to be their first ruler. Saul started well, but like the Israelites themselves, soon lost his way . . .

Judges; 1 Samuel

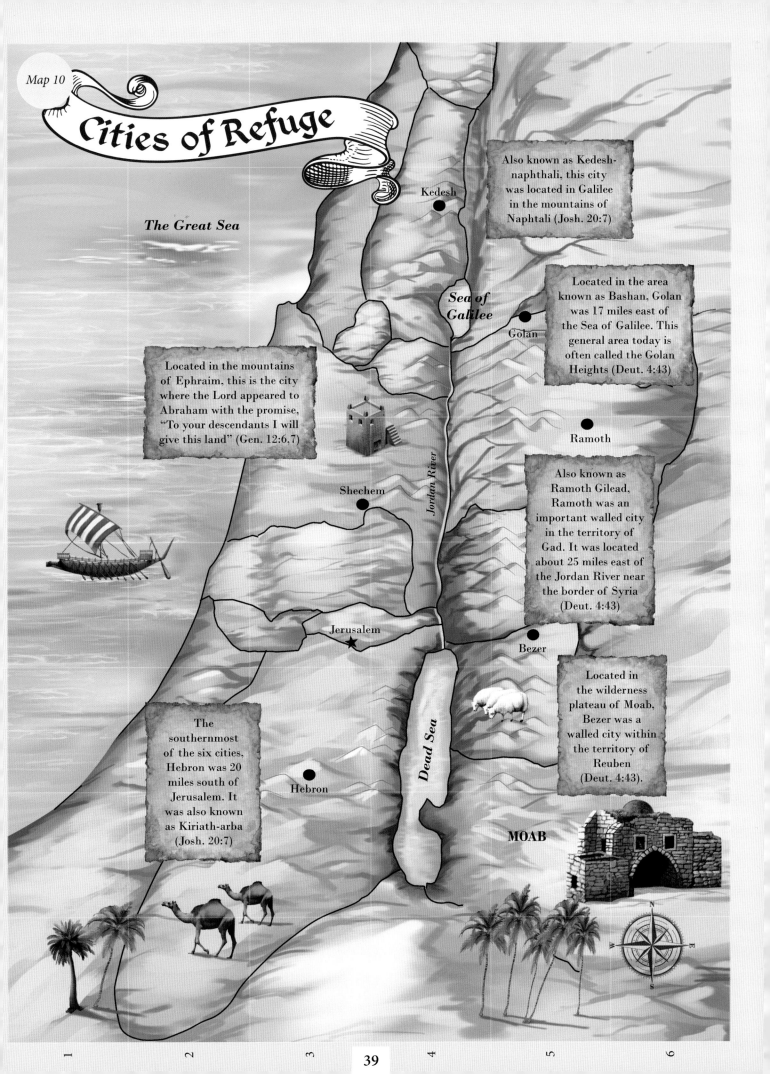

Map 10

Cities of Refuge

The Great Sea

Kedesh

Also known as Kedesh-naphthali, this city was located in Galilee in the mountains of Naphtali (Josh. 20:7)

Sea of Galilee

Located in the area known as Bashan, Golan was 17 miles east of the Sea of Galilee. This general area today is often called the Golan Heights (Deut. 4:43)

Golan

Located in the mountains of Ephraim, this is the city where the Lord appeared to Abraham with the promise, "To your descendants I will give this land" (Gen. 12:6,7)

Ramoth

Jordan River

Shechem

Also known as Ramoth Gilead, Ramoth was an important walled city in the territory of Gad. It was located about 25 miles east of the Jordan River near the border of Syria (Deut. 4:43)

Jerusalem

Bezer

Located in the wilderness plateau of Moab, Bezer was a walled city within the territory of Reuben (Deut. 4:43).

Dead Sea

The southernmost of the six cities, Hebron was 20 miles south of Jerusalem. It was also known as Kiriath-arba (Josh. 20:7)

Hebron

MOAB

1   2   3   4   5   6

SAUL IS IMPATIENT

Saul became a mighty king and had many victories over the Philistines. To begin with, he was good and brave, but over time, Saul became proud and obstinate, and he didn't always obey God.

Once, Saul and his army were waiting at Gilgal, preparing to fight the Philistines and dreadfully outnumbered. Samuel had promised to meet them there to offer a sacrifice before going to war, but Saul and his soldiers were quaking with fear, and day after day Samuel didn't come. When Saul's soldiers began to desert, he decided to make the offering himself.

Samuel arrived just as he finished. He was angry and told Saul that because he had disobeyed God, his sons would not rule the country after him. Instead God would choose another king.

1 Samuel 13

Map 12
E4

THE DISOBEDIENT KING

Some years later, God told Saul to attack the Amalekites and to destroy Amalek and everything in it. Saul killed all the people, but he spared the best of the animals and took the king as a hostage.

When Samuel asked Saul why he had disobeyed God, Saul told him that he was planning to sacrifice the animals to the Lord. "God wants you to obey him!" said Samuel. "He didn't ask for sacrifices!"

Saul begged for forgiveness and grabbed hold of Samuel's robe to stop him leaving. A corner of it tore off in his hands! Samuel told him that just as Saul had torn his cloak, the Lord would tear the kingdom away from Saul, for God regretted that he had ever made him king over Israel. Samuel left and never saw Saul again.

1 Samuel 15

Map 1.
C2

Map 12
C3

THE SHEPHERD BOY

Samuel went to the house of Jesse in Bethlehem, for God had chosen one of his sons to be king of Israel. One by one, Jesse brought out his sons, all strong and handsome. Samuel thought they seemed fine young men, but not one of them was the chosen one, for God looks at the inside of a person, not the outside.

Samuel asked if there were any more sons, and Jesse answered, "There is the youngest, David, but he is tending the sheep in the fields."

When the young shepherd boy was brought before Samuel, the Lord spoke, "This is the one I have chosen!"

Samuel anointed him then and there, but it was some time yet before David would be king. For now, he stayed at home tending the sheep, playing his harp, and practicing with his sling. But from that day onward, God was always with him.

1 Samuel 16

DAVID AND GOLIATH

The Israelites were at war with the Philistines, and the two armies had gathered to do battle. David had brought food to his brothers who were fighting in the army.

The Philistines had a mighty champion. His name was Goliath, and he was powerful and strong—and ten feet tall! Goliath had challenged the Israelite soldiers to single combat. Not one of them had dared to fight this terrible warrior. But David was not afraid—he told Saul that he would fight Goliath, for God had been with him when he had protected his sheep from lions and bears, and David knew that God would be with him now.

1 Samuel 17

A STONE IN A SLING

The king gave David his own armor and weapons, but David did not feel comfortable using them. Instead he stood before Goliath with nothing but his staff, a sling, and five smooth stones.

Goliath laughed when he saw the young shepherd boy, but David fearlessly ran toward him, putting a stone in his sling and flinging it with all his might. It hit Goliath right in the middle of his forehead, and when he fell to the ground, David raced up and, drawing out Goliath's own sword, cut his head from his body with one strike!

The Philistines were so shocked when they saw their champion killed that they turned and fled!

1 Samuel 17

Map 11
C-D2

DAVID BECOMES KING

David did not become king immediately. First he served King Saul as a musician and as his armor-bearer, and became very close to Saul's son Jonathan. David grew to be a great warrior and was very popular with the people. Saul became very jealous. Several times he tried to kill David, but God always protected him.

Many years later, Jonathan was killed fighting against the Philistines in a huge battle, and Saul took his own life the same day. David was filled with sorrow when he learned of their deaths. Saul's only remaining son, Ish-bosheth, was proclaimed king over all the northern part of Israel by Saul's general, Abner, but the tribe of Judah remained loyal to David, and for some time there was bitter fighting between Ish-bosheth's army and David's followers.

But finally, after much much bloodshed, the conflict was over and David was proclaimed king over all Israel.

1-2 Samuel

THE WATER TUNNEL

As one of his first acts as king, David decided to make the fortress city of Jerusalem his new capital, for he knew that the enemies of Israel were always waiting to pounce.

He marched his army to Jerusalem, which was still held by a Canaanite tribe. The people there laughed at him, believing that they would be safe behind their high walls. Hills surrounded the city on three sides, and the fourth was protected by the huge city gates. "You'll never get inside," they taunted. "The blind and the lame could defend us!"

But David had God's blessing. He discovered that a water tunnel ran up through the hill to the city. His men climbed up the water shaft, right into the heart of the city, and unlocked the gates from the inside, and so the mighty fortress fell to David and his soldiers!

2 Samuel 5

THE ARK IS BROUGHT TO JERUSALEM

Once David had conquered the city, he sent for carpenters and stonemasons to enlarge it and to build a grand palace. Jerusalem became known as David's city. But David knew he owed everything to God. He wanted Jerusalem to be known as God's city, so he had the Ark of the Covenant brought to Jerusalem.

There was great rejoicing when the Ark entered the city. David was beside himself with happiness and sang and danced along with all his people. His new wife thought he was making a fool of himself. "How could you embarrass yourself so?" she asked him later.

She didn't understand that David didn't care about his own dignity, but thought only of praising God.

2 Samuel 6;
1 Chronicles 13; 15-16

Map 11
D3

DAVID AND BATHSHEBA

One evening David was walking on the palace roof when his eyes were drawn to a beautiful woman bathing. His guards told him it was Bathsheba, the wife of one of his soldiers, Uriah, who was away fighting the Ammonites. David was filled with love for Bathsheba and had her brought to the palace that night. Soon afterward he learned that she was expecting his child!

David knew Uriah would be furious if he learned the truth, so he brought him home to be with his wife, hoping he would believe the baby was his own. But when Uriah insisted on sleeping by the palace gates, David sent him back to the front line where the fighting was fiercest, and he was killed. At the end of Bathsheba's mourning period, David married her, and she bore him a son.

God was not pleased. He sent the prophet Nathan to David to explain how wicked he had been, and David was filled with remorse and repented. God forgave him, and although that child did not live, in time Bathsheba gave David another child, a son named Solomon, and Solomon was loved by God.

2 Samuel 11

SOLOMON BECOMES KING

David was old and on his deathbed, and his sons were fighting over the throne. He had promised it to Solomon, but another of his sons, Adonijah, wanted to be king himself and tried to claim the throne. The prophet Nathan learned what was happening, and he and Bathsheba went to tell David the news.

The king told Bathsheba to arrange for Solomon to ride David's own mule to Gihon, where Nathan and Zadok the priest were to anoint him king over Israel. "Blow the trumpet and shout, 'Long live King Solomon!'" commanded David, "for he is to come and sit on my throne and reign in my place."

When Adonijah heard the people had learned what had happened, he was terrified his brother would kill him. But Solomon sent word to him: "As long as you do no evil, you will live," and Adonijah returned home in relief.

1 Kings 1–2; 1 Chronicles 29

GOD SPEAKS TO SOLOMON

Soon after Solomon had been crowned king, God spoke to him in a dream. "What would you like me to give you, Solomon?" he said. "Ask for whatever you want."

Solomon thought for a moment and then answered humbly, "I'm young and have no experience. Please give me wisdom that I might rule over your people wisely and do as you would have me do. Help me to distinguish between what is right and what is wrong."

God was pleased with Solomon's answer. "I will give you wisdom. But I will also give you those things you did not ask for. You will be rich and respected, and if you follow in my ways, you will live a long and good life." Solomon awoke feeling comforted and strengthened.

1 Kings 3; 2 Chronicles 1

Map 11
D3

THE WISDOM OF SOLOMON

Two women came before Solomon, holding a baby between them. "My lord," said one, "this woman and I live in the same house, and we both bore babies at the same time. But her baby died in the night, and she took my son from my side and replaced him with her dead son!"

The other woman said, "You are lying! The living one is my son; the dead one is yours." And so they argued.

Solomon ordered a guard, "Cut the child in two and give half to one woman and half to the other."

One woman cried out in horror. "No! Give her the baby! I would rather she looked after him than he died!" But the other woman said that they should do as the king commanded, for that would be fair.

Then the king gave his ruling: "Give the baby to the first woman. Don't kill him; she is his true mother." When people heard about the verdict the king had given, they saw how wise and clever God had made him.

1 Kings 3

Map 11
D3

BUILDING THE TEMPLE

Years before, King David had hoped to build a special temple for the Ark of the Covenant. But God had told him not to. Instead, the task fell to David's son Solomon.

Not long after he had been made king, Solomon began work on the temple. He sent for the finest cedar wood, and the stones were cut at the quarry, so that hammers and chisels would not be heard on the holy site.

The temple was wide and long and tall, with many chambers, and the most sacred of all was the Most Holy Place. Here, the fine cedar was sculpted into beautiful shapes and forms, and the doors were exquisitely carved and covered in fine gold.

The temple took thousands of men seven years to build, and when it was finished, King Solomon filled it with fine treasures. But the finest treasure of all was the Ark of the Covenant, containing the two stone tablets. It was brought to lie in the Most Holy Place, where it rested under the wings of two cherubim made of olive wood and covered in gold, each fifteen feet high, their wings touching in the middle of the room.

The cloud of God's presence filled the temple, and the people were full of wonder and thankfulness. Then Solomon thanked God. "I know that you who created heaven and earth would never live in a building made by man, but I pray that here we can be close to you and hear your word."

God told him that he had heard his prayer, that his heart and eyes would be in the temple, and that as long as the king walked in God's ways and kept his laws, he would be with him.

1 Kings 5-8; 2 Chronicles 2-7

THE QUEEN OF SHEBA

Solomon grew very rich. After he had built the sacred temple, he built magnificent palaces for himself and one of his wives. He ate off gold plates using gold cutlery and drank from a golden goblet. Even the clothes he wore were threaded with gold.

The stories of his wealth and wisdom traveled far and wide. The Queen of Sheba came to visit from her kingdom far away. She arrived with a long caravan of camels carrying rare spices, gold, and precious stones as gifts.

She asked Solomon many questions, and every question was answered wisely and clearly. "Everything I heard was true!" she told the king. "I thought that people were exaggerating, but now I know they were not. Your people must be proud to have you as their ruler, and it is a sign of your God's love for them that he has made you their king, to rule them with justice and wisdom."

1 Kings 10; 2 Chronicles 9

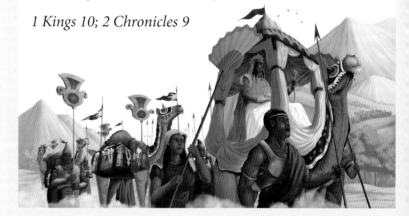

KING DAVID

David was the second king of the united kingdom of Israel and Judah, and he reigned around 1010–970 BC.

A brave warrior and the poet and musician credited for composing many psalms in the book of Psalms, King David is widely considered as a righteous and effective king in battle as well as in civil and criminal justice.

Jesus was a descendant of David.

KING SOLOMON

Solomon was tremendously wealthy and was a wise king of Israel. He was a son of King David and built the first temple in Jerusalem.

Solomon is portrayed throughout the books of Kings and Chronicles as being greater than all his predecessors in terms of wisdom, wealth, and power.

Ultimately, however, he was a human being, with failings that led him into sin. Solomon's sins led to the division of the kingdom during the reign of Rehoboam, his son.

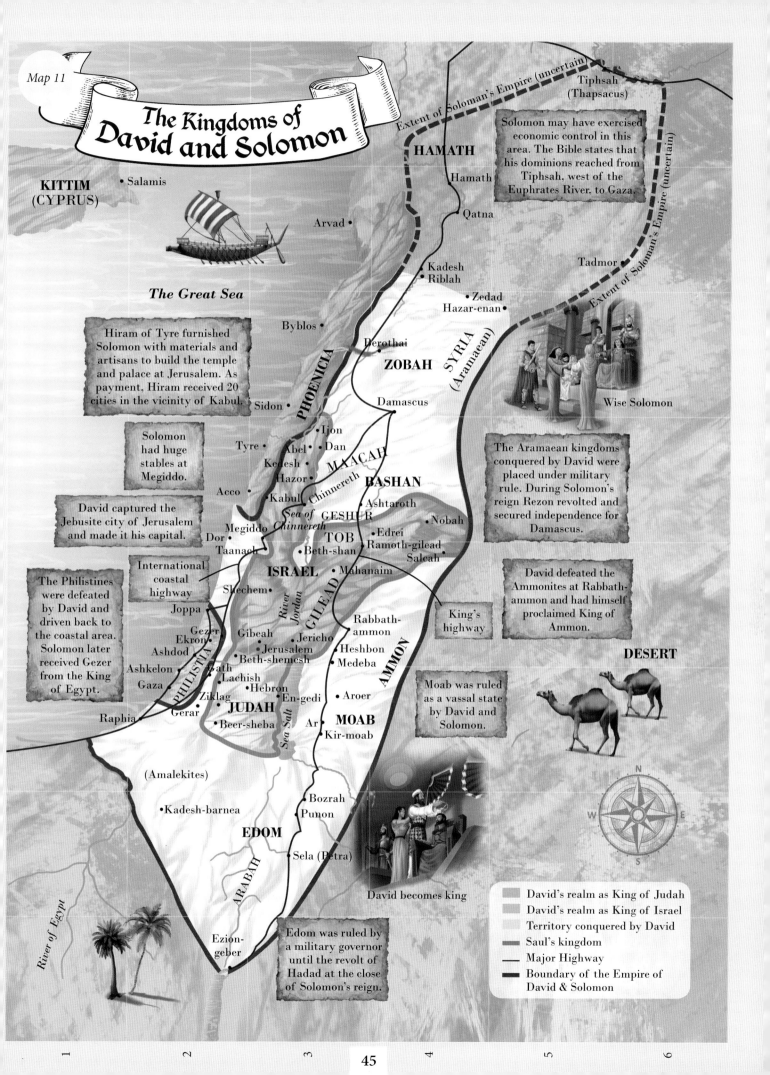

Map 11

The Kingdoms of David and Solomon

KITTIM (CYPRUS)

• Salamis

The Great Sea

HAMATH

Hamath

Qatna

Solomon may have exercised economic control in this area. The Bible states that his dominions reached from Tiphsah, west of the Euphrates River, to Gaza.

Tiphsah (Thapsacus)

Extent of Soloman's Empire (uncertain)

Extent of Soloman's Empire (uncertain)

Arvad •

Kadesh
• Riblah

Tadmor

• Zedad
Hazar-enan •

Byblos •

Berothai •

ZOBAH

SYRIA (Aramaean)

Hiram of Tyre furnished Solomon with materials and artisans to build the temple and palace at Jerusalem. As payment, Hiram received 20 cities in the vicinity of Kabul.

Sidon •

PHOENICIA

Damascus •

Wise Solomon

• Ijon

Solomon had huge stables at Megiddo.

Tyre •
Abel • • Dan
Kedesh •

MAACAH

Hazor •

BASHAN

The Aramaean kingdoms conquered by David were placed under military rule. During Solomon's reign Rezon revolted and secured independence for Damascus.

Acco •
Kabul • Chinnereth
Sea of Chinnereth
• Ashtaroth

• Nobah

David captured the Jebusite city of Jerusalem and made it his capital.

Megiddo •
Dor •
Taanach •

GESHUR

TOB

• Edrei
Ramoth-gilead •
Salcah •

International coastal highway

ISRAEL

• Beth-shan

• Mahanaim

David defeated the Ammonites at Rabbath-ammon and had himself proclaimed King of Ammon.

Shechem •

GILEAD

River Jordan

The Philistines were defeated by David and driven back to the coastal area. Solomon later received Gezer from the King of Egypt.

Joppa •

Gezer •
Ekron •
Gibeah •
• Jericho

Rabbath-ammon

King's highway

Ashdod •
• Beth-shemesh
Ashkelon •
Gath •
Gaza •
Lachish •
Ziklag •
Gerar •

PHILISTIA

• Jerusalem

Heshbon •
Medeba •

AMMON

DESERT

Raphia •

• Hebron
• En-gedi

Sea Salt

• Aroer

Moab was ruled as a vassal state by David and Solomon.

JUDAH
• Beer-sheba

Ar • **MOAB**
• Kir-moab

(Amalekites)

•Kadesh-barnea

• Bozrah
Punon •

EDOM

River of Egypt

ARABAH

• Sela (Petra)

David becomes king

Ezion-geber

Edom was ruled by a military governor until the revolt of Hadad at the close of Solomon's reign.

	David's realm as King of Judah
	David's realm as King of Israel
	Territory conquered by David
—	Saul's kingdom
—	Major Highway
—	Boundary of the Empire of David & Solomon

1   2   3   4   5   6

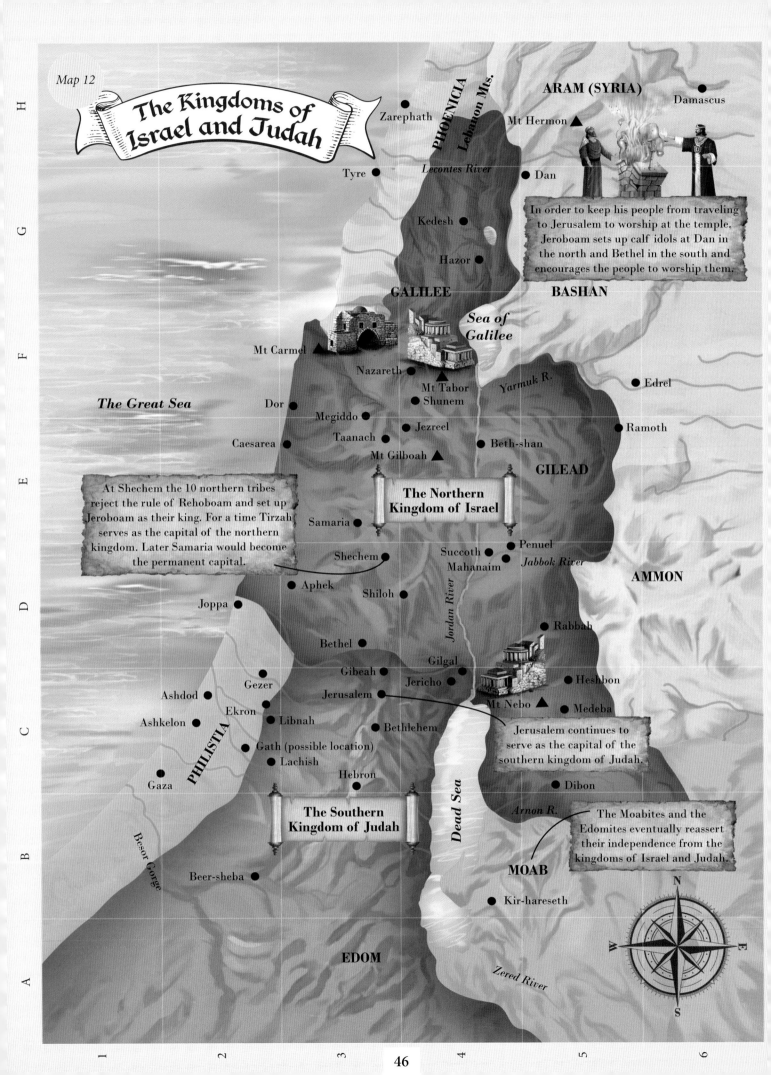

Map 12

The Kingdoms of Israel and Judah

ARAM (SYRIA)

Damascus

Zarephath

PHOENICIA

Lebanon Mts.

Mt Hermon ▲

Lecontes River

Tyre

Dan

In order to keep his people from traveling to Jerusalem to worship at the temple, Jeroboam sets up calf idols at Dan in the north and Bethel in the south and encourages the people to worship them.

Kedesh

Hazor

GALILEE

BASHAN

Sea of Galilee

Mt Carmel ▲

Nazareth

Mt Tabor ▲

The Great Sea

Shunem

Yarmuk R.

Edrel

Dor

Megiddo

Jezreel

Ramoth

Taanach

Caesarea

Beth-shan

Mt Gilboah ▲

GILEAD

At Shechem the 10 northern tribes reject the rule of Rehoboam and set up Jeroboam as their king. For a time Tirzah serves as the capital of the northern kingdom. Later Samaria would become the permanent capital.

The Northern Kingdom of Israel

Samaria

Penuel

Succoth

Jabbok River

Mahanaim

AMMON

Shechem

Aphek

Shiloh

Jordan River

Joppa

Rabbah

Bethel

Gilgal

Gibeah

Jericho

Heshbon

Gezer

Jerusalem

Ashdod

Ekron

Libnah

Mt Nebo ▲

Medeba

Ashkelon

PHILISTIA

Bethlehem

Jerusalem continues to serve as the capital of the southern kingdom of Judah.

Gath (possible location)

Lachish

Hebron

Dibon

Gaza

The Southern Kingdom of Judah

Arnon R.

The Moabites and the Edomites eventually reassert their independence from the kingdoms of Israel and Judah.

MOAB

Besor Gorge

Beer-sheba

Dead Sea

Kir-hareseth

N

EDOM

Zered River

W E

S

46

TURNING FROM GOD

Solomon was greater and richer than any other king, yet when he grew old, he turned from God, influenced by the foreign wives he had married. God was angry and sad, but for the sake of David, he didn't take the kingdom in Solomon's own lifetime.

One day the prophet Ahijah came to Jeroboam, one of the king's officials. Ahijah tore his cloak into twelve pieces and gave ten to Jeroboam, saying, "Soon God will take away ten tribes from Solomon and give them to you. God will punish Solomon and Israel because they have forsaken him, but he won't take away all the kingdom from David's children; he will give them the tribes of Judah and Benjamin. And if you serve God truly, he will give your kingdom to your sons after you."

Jeroboam went to Egypt, where he stayed until Solomon died, and then the kingdom of Israel split in two. In the south, the tribes of Judah and Benjamin stayed loyal to Solomon's son, King Rehoboam, but the ten northern tribes broke away and made Jeroboam their king.

1 Kings 11

Map 12

ISRAEL IS DIVIDED

Despite Ahijah's message, Jeroboam didn't follow God's laws. He had two calves made out of gold for the people to worship, for he was worried that if they traveled to Jerusalem to worship at the holy temple there, they might go back to King Rehoboam.

God sent a holy man to deliver a message. He came to the king at one of the altars and told him God would send a sign: The altar would split open and ashes rain down. Jeroboam was furious. He stretched out his hand to tell his guards to seize the man, and as he did so his hand shriveled up, the altar was split apart, and its ashes poured out. Yet even after this dire warning, Jeroboam still didn't change his ways!

Nor was King Rehoboam in the south much better, for he too had let his people return to the wicked ways of the tribes who had lived in this land before them.

1 Kings 12-14; 2 Chronicles 10-12

For much of the existence of Israel, and the kingdoms of Judah and Israel, Moab and Edom were vassal states, subordinate to the conquering nations. Eventually, both revolted and regained their independence.

CAPTURED BY ASSYRIA

The years passed, and Israel fell into disgrace. Its kings were rotten, and the people turned from God to worship Baal and other false idols. God was sad that his people had turned away from him. He had done so much for them—he had saved them from slavery and had brought them to this beautiful land—but they had fallen into wicked ways and had not listened to the warnings of the prophets that he had sent them.

So when the great armies of Assyria came, Israel fell, for it was time for God to punish his children. For nearly three years the armies of Assyria laid siege to the city of Samaria, and at last it fell. Then the Israelites were forced to leave their country and made to march to a far-off land, and new people came to live in Samaria, bringing their false gods with them.

2 Kings 17

JEREMIAH IS CALLED

One of the greatest prophets of the Lord was Jeremiah. God showed Jeremiah a large cooking pot over a blazing fire. As Jeremiah watched, the liquid in the pot began to boil, spilling over in a huge rush of steaming liquid.

"In just such a way will an enemy from the north spill over into the lands of Judah and Jerusalem, and destroy all that lies in its path," warned God. "Warn the people so that they mend their ways."

The people didn't like what Jeremiah had to say, but still he passed on God's messages.

Jeremiah 1

THE FALL OF JERUSALEM

The latest king of Judah, Zedekiah, tried to rebel against Nebuchadnezzar, despite the warnings of Jeremiah, and the mighty forces of Babylon came and camped outside Jerusalem. Zedekiah was terrified. He begged Jeremiah for advice, and Jeremiah told him, "God says, 'If you surrender, your life will be spared and the city won't be burned down. But if you won't, the city will be given to the Babylonians, they will burn it down, and you won't escape.'"

Even now, Zedekiah would not listen to Jeremiah. He tried to flee in the middle of the night. But the Babylonians cut them down and then destroyed the city utterly. They set fire to the temple, the palace, and all the houses, and the rest of the people were taken away as slaves. They had refused to listen to God, and now they were being punished.

2 Kings 25; 2 Chronicles 36

CONQUERED

For too long the people of Judah ignored God's warnings. It was time for them to be punished. Just as Jeremiah had warned, Jerusalem fell to mighty Nebuchadnezzar and his army, who set up a puppet king and sent all the strong, skilled people away to Babylon. Jeremiah wrote a letter to comfort them and give them hope:

"God says: 'When seventy years are completed, I will bring you back. You will pray to me, and I will listen. You will seek me and find me when you seek with all your heart, and I will bring you back from captivity.'"

Jeremiah 29

Map 12
C3

COMFORT IN DESPAIR

Jerusalem was destroyed. Years before, the prophet Isaiah had known this would happen, and had a message of hope for the exiles from God: "'Comfort my people,' says your God. 'Speak tenderly to Jerusalem, and tell her she has paid for her sins.'

"God tends his flock like a shepherd. He gathers the lambs and carries them close to his heart. So never believe he doesn't care about you. God gives strength and power to those who need it. Those who place their trust in God will soar on wings like eagles."

God knew his children would learn from their lesson, and then they would return home with God by their side. But for now, they were slaves in a foreign country.

Isaiah 40

VEGETABLES AND WATER

Daniel was an exile living in Babylon, but because he came from a good family, he had been chosen to live in the royal palace, where he and his three friends were well-treated and given a good education. Daniel asked if he and his friends might have vegetables and water instead of the king's food and wine, for God had forbidden certain foods. The steward worried that they would become weak, but Daniel persuaded the guard to given them vegetables and water for ten days and then see how they looked. When they became healthier and fitter than the other young men, they were allowed to continue.

After three years they were the cleverest and wisest of all the students. Daniel could even understand dreams. So it was that they were chosen to be advisors to the king himself.

Daniel 1

Map 13
F5

THE MYSTERIOUS DREAM

Not long after this, the king began having the same dream over and over again. He was so worried that he called all his fortune-tellers and wizards to him, saying, "My dream is worrying me. Tell me what it means."

His advisors looked puzzled. They asked him to describe the dream, but the king wanted them to work it out themselves and then tell him the meaning. "What you ask is impossible! Only the gods could do this!" exclaimed the wizards.

The king was so furious that he ordered all his advisors executed, including Daniel and his friends! But Daniel begged for time to interpret the dream, and then he and his friends prayed to God. That night, the mystery was revealed to him.

Daniel 2

THE DREAM EXPLAINED

The next day, he explained that it foretold the future: "You saw a terrible and massive statue. Its head was made of gold, its chest and arms of silver, its waist and hips of bronze, its legs of iron, and its feet partly of iron and partly of clay. While you watched, a great stone fell, smashing into its feet and shattering them. Then the statue crumbled, disappearing into dust borne away by the wind. But the stone grew into a mountain that covered the earth.

"This is what it means. The mighty kingdom of Babylon is the gold head, and the other parts of the statue are empires yet to come. There will be another empire, then another, which will rule the whole earth. Then yet another empire will emerge, as strong as iron, crushing all the earlier ones. Yet it will be divided, for the feet were made of iron and of clay. But God will establish another kingdom that will never be conquered and that will destroy all those before it. God's kingdom will never end. That is the stone that will become a mountain."

The impressed king declared that Daniel's God truly was the wisest and greatest, and he made Daniel his chief advisor.

Daniel 2

49

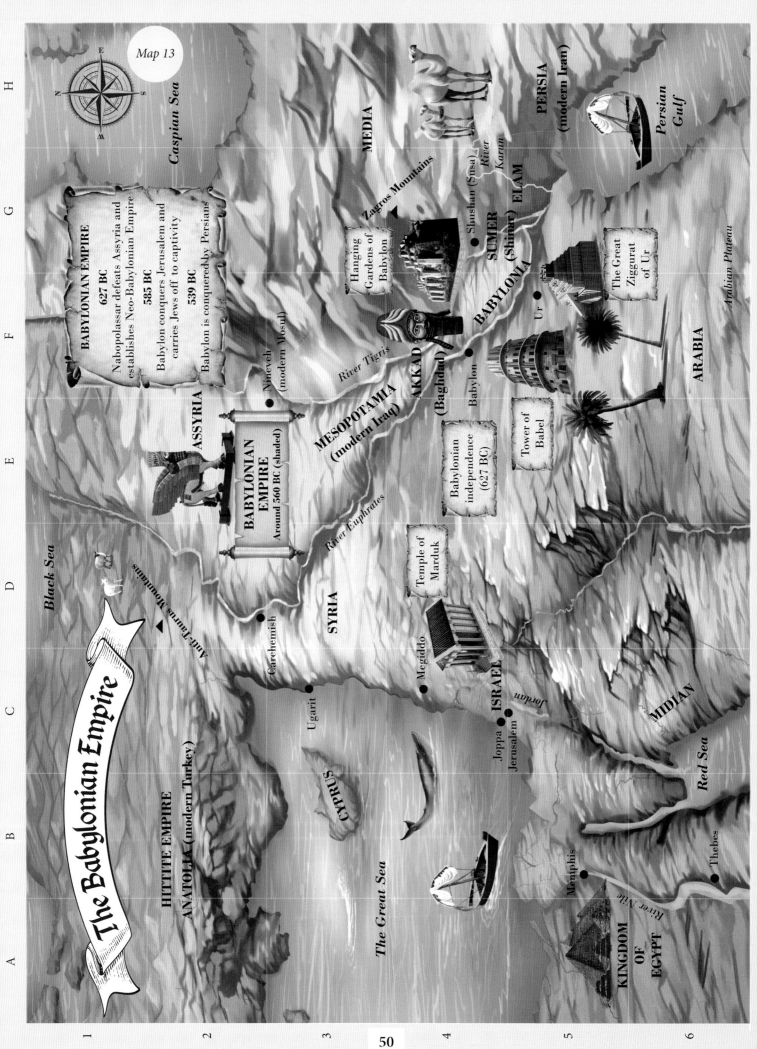

Map 13

The Babylonian Empire

Black Sea

Caspian Sea

HITTITE EMPIRE
ANATOLIA (modern Turkey)

Anti-Taurus Mountains

BABYLONIAN EMPIRE

627 BC
Nabopolassar defeats Assyria and establishes Neo-Babylonian Empire

585 BC
Babylon conquers Jerusalem and carries off Jews to captivity

539 BC
Babylon is conquered by Persians

ASSYRIA

Nineveh (modern Mosul)

River Tigris

BABYLONIAN EMPIRE
Around 560 BC (shaded)

MEDIA

Hanging Gardens of Babylon

Zagros Mountains

Slushan (Susa)

River Karun

PERSIA (modern Iran)

Persian Gulf

SUMER (Shinar) ELAM

AKKAD (Baghdad)

BABYLONIA

Babylon

Babylonian independence (627 BC)

Tower of Babel

Ur

The Great Ziggurat of Ur

Arabian Plateau

ARABIA

River Euphrates

Temple of Marduk

SYRIA

Carchemish

Ugarit

Megiddo

Joppa
Jerusalem

ISRAEL

Jordan

CYPRUS

MIDIAN

Red Sea

The Great Sea

Memphis

Thebes

KINGDOM OF EGYPT

River Nile

50

THE GREAT ZIGGURAT OF UR

Map 13 F5

The Great Ziggurat of Ur was built in the Early Bronze Age (twenty-first century BC) in honor of the moon god, Sin. Ziggurats were huge structures built in the Mesopotamian valley and western Iranian plateau. These terraced step pyramids were topped with a shrine and were believed to bring people both physically and spiritually closer to God.

THE HANGING GARDENS OF BABYLON

It is believed that the Babylonian king Nebuchadnezzar II built the Hanging Gardens for his wife, Amytis, who was homesick for the green, mountainous terrain of her homeland in the Median Empire. In order to please his wife, the king ordered the construction of the celebrated tiered gardens containing all manner of trees, shrubs, and vines. The Hanging Gardens of Babylon were one of the Seven Wonders of the Ancient World.

Map 13 F5

THE TOWER OF BABEL

The Tower of Babel was built by Noah's descendants, who wanted to create a tower tall enough to reach heaven. Because of their arrogance and pride, God made them unable to speak to each other, and so the tower was left unfinished.

According to ancient accounts, Babylonian temple towers were square or rectangular and built upward in stages.

THE TEMPLE OF MARDUK

The temple of Marduk, also called the Ésagila, was dedicated to Marduk, the protector god of Babylon. It was, after the Ziggurat and the royal Palace, the greatest of the architectural complexes of Babylon. Its large court contained a smaller court, a central shrine, huge square towers, and crenellated terraces.

Map 13 F5

THE WRITING ON THE WALL

When Nebuchadnezzar's grandson, Belshazzar, was king, he held a grand banquet and sent for the gold and silver goblets taken from the holy temple in Jerusalem. He and his guests drank wine out of them as they praised the false idols they had created. Suddenly the fingers of a human hand appeared and began to write on the plaster of the wall. The king turned white with terror and began to shake. He asked his advisors what the strange writing meant, but not one of them had a clue.

Finally he sent for Daniel, who explained the writing with God's help: "King Nebuchadnezzar was mighty and proud, but he learned that God alone rules over this world and chooses who shall be king. You have not learned this lesson. Your heart is hard, and you are full of pride. You don't honor God, who has given you all you have, but use goblets taken from God's holy temple and bow down before false idols.

"This hand was sent by God. He has written, 'Mene, Mene, Tekel, Parsin,' and this is what it means: Mene—the days of your kingdom have been numbered; Tekel—you have been weighed on the scales and found wanting; Parsin—your kingdom will be divided."

That very night, Belshazzar was killed and Darius the Mede took over the kingdom.

Daniel 5

Map 13 F5

THE SNEAKY TRAP

Darius was impressed with Daniel, for he was wise and honest, and soon Darius put him in charge of his whole kingdom. The other officials were jealous. They knew Daniel prayed to his God every day at his window, and they came up with a plan.

"Your Majesty," said one of them. "We have written a new law. It states that for the next thirty days, whoever asks anything of any god or any man, except of you, our king, shall be thrown into a den of lions. Please sign your name to the decree so that it is official and cannot be changed." So the king signed his name, for he didn't realize that they were setting a trap for Daniel!

Daniel continued to pray just as he had always done. He would not stop praying to God or even hide what he was doing. His enemies told the king that Daniel was breaking the law and demanded that Daniel be thrown to the lions. Darius was sad, but he had no alternative.

Daniel 6

DANIEL IN THE LIONS' DEN

That evening the king didn't sleep a wink. At first light, he rushed down to the pit. "Daniel!" he cried out, more in desperation than hope. "Has your God been able to save you?"

He could not believe his ears when Daniel answered, "My God sent an angel and shut the mouths of the lions. They have not hurt me, for I was found innocent. Nor have I ever wronged you." The king was overjoyed and had Daniel brought out immediately. Then he ordered the men who had tricked him to be thrown into the pit themselves—and this time the lions were ruthless!

After this, Darius ordered his people to respect and honor Daniel's God, "For he can do wonderful things in heaven and on earth, and he rescued Daniel from the power of the lions!"

Daniel 6

Map 13
F5

RETURN TO JERUSALEM

When Daniel was an old man, King Cyrus took the throne. His Persian empire stretched far and wide, but God touched his heart, and the mighty king issued a decree that the exiles from Judah could at last return home. He also sent for the precious treasures taken from God's temple so many years ago and gave them to the exiles to take back.

Great was the excitement and the rejoicing among the people. They couldn't believe that they were finally going to return home! But not everybody was able to return to Jerusalem. The journey would be long and hard, and it would take time to rebuild the temple and city. Only the strongest and fittest were able to go.

Daniel was one of those who stayed behind. But his heart was filled with joy as he saw his people set out on their way, singing praises to God and laughing and smiling, and he gave thanks to God for allowing his people to return home and start again.

Ezra 1

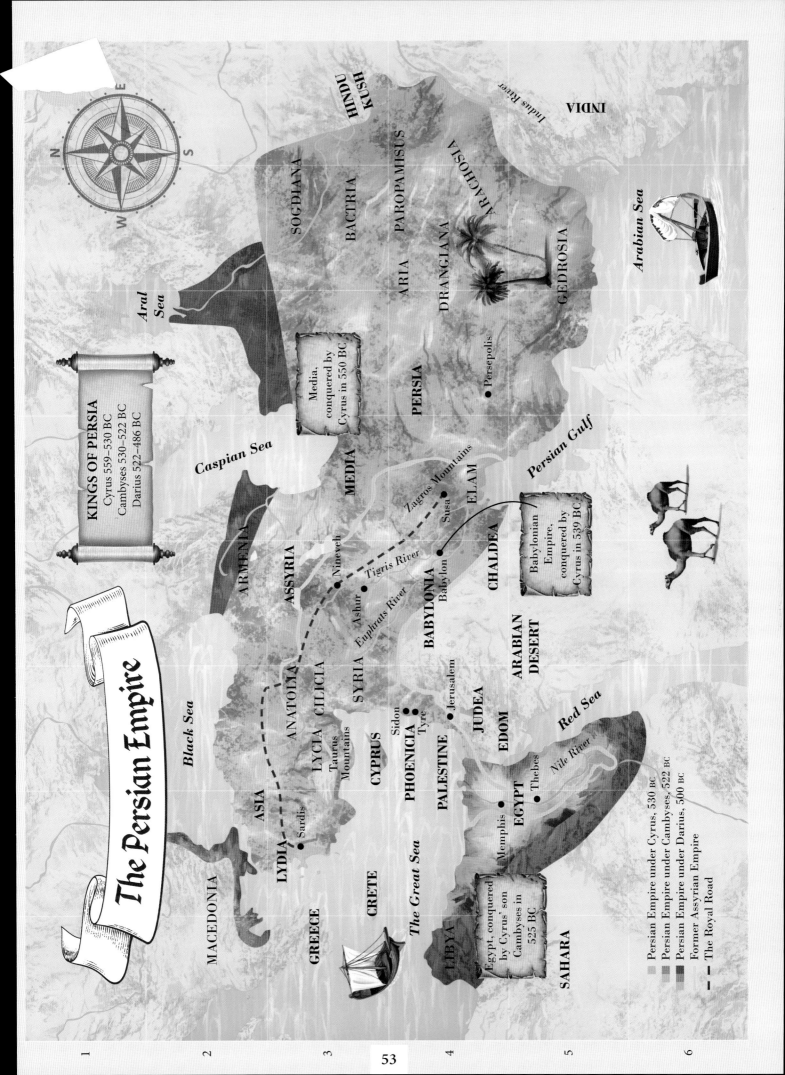

The Persian Empire

KINGS OF PERSIA
Cyrus 559–530 BC
Cambyses 530–522 BC
Darius 522–486 BC

Media, conquered by Cyrus in 550 BC

Babylonian Empire, conquered by Cyrus in 539 BC

Egypt, conquered by Cyrus' son Cambyses in 525 BC

Persian Empire under Cyrus, 530 BC
Persian Empire under Cambyses, 522 BC
Persian Empire under Darius, 500 BC
Former Assyrian Empire
The Royal Road

INDIA
HINDU KUSH
Indus River
SOGDIANA
BACTRIA
PAROPAMISUS
ARACHOSIA
ARIA
DRANGIANA
GEDROSIA
Arabian Sea
Aral Sea
Persepolis
PERSIA
MEDIA
Caspian Sea
Persian Gulf
Zagros Mountains
Susa
ELAM
CHALDEA
Nineveh
Tigris River
Ashur
Euphrats River
Babylon
BABYLONIA
ARMENIA
ASSYRIA
ANATOLIA
CILICIA
LYCIA
SYRIA
Sidon
PHOENICIA
Tyre
CYPRUS
Jerusalem
JUDEA
ARABIAN DESERT
Taurus Mountains
ASIA
LYDIA
Sardis
Black Sea
PALESTINE
EDOM
Red Sea
Nile River
Memphis
EGYPT
Thebes
MACEDONIA
GREECE
CRETE
The Great Sea
LIBYA
SAHARA

1
2
3
53
4
5
6

THE ANGRY KING

King Xerxes was the new ruler of Persia. Annoyed with his wife, Queen Vashti, for her disobedience, he sent her away, and so he needed a new queen. He sent for all the beautiful maidens of the land to come to the capital in Susa, and from them chose a lovely girl named Esther.

Esther's cousin Mordecai warned her not to tell her new husband that she was a Jew. Mordecai himself came to work at the palace and managed to stop an assassination attempt on the king when he overheard a secret conversation. What had happened and Mordecai's part in it was written down in the official records, but the king forgot to reward the man who had saved his life!

Esther 1-2

THE BRAVE QUEEN

The king's prime minister, Haman, was furious when Mordecai refused to bow to him. When he found out that Mordecai was a Jew, he decided to punish not only him, but all Jews. He told the king that there was a race of people in his empire that did not obey his laws, and he persuaded the king to sign a decree stating that on a specific day, all the Jews in the empire were to be killed!

When Mordecai learned of the decree, he begged Esther to plead their case before the king. Esther was terrified. To go before the king without a summons was punishable by death, but Mordecai told her that maybe God had made her queen precisely so that she could save his people, and so she plucked up her courage.

When Xerxes saw her, he smiled and said, "Tell me what you want, and you shall have it!" Esther dared not ask him then, but invited him and Haman to a banquet.

Esther 3-5

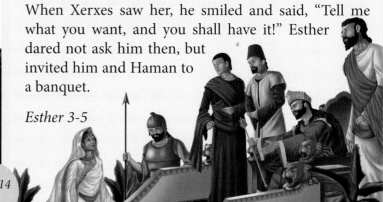

Map 14
E4

HAMAN IS PUNISHED

The following day, Haman, angry at Mordecai's refusal to bow, decided that he would arrange to have the man executed, and that night he went to ask the king for his permission. But when he spoke to the king, he was horrified to learn that the king wished to honor Mordecai, having found out how he had saved his life in the past.

At the queen's banquet, things only got worse, for brave Esther finally told the king that someone had arranged for the slaughter of her people, and she begged him to save them. When Xerxes found out that Haman was responsible, he ordered his execution on the spot.

Esther 5-7

ARM YOURSELVES!

However, the danger was not over, for a decree stamped with the royal seal could not be changed. But the king sent out another proclamation, stating that all Jews might arm themselves, and if attacked, might fight back and destroy the attackers and take all their possessions.

So when the followers of Haman tried to massacre the Jewish people, the Jews fought back and destroyed them. Haman's sons were hanged, and throughout the land the enemies of the Jews were destroyed. The Jewish people were saved from annihilation, and every year Jews celebrate the festival of Purim in remembrance and gratitude.

Esther 8-9

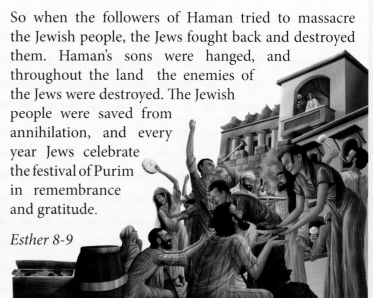

THE TASK AHEAD

Rebuilding Jerusalem was a hard and long task. When the first exiles returned, the walls and buildings were ruined, and the holy temple was no more than a pile of rubble. They put up an altar where the temple had once stood so they could worship God properly, but some became disheartened at the task ahead, and when the locals made things difficult for them, work came to a halt.

But God sent prophets to encourage his people, and work started on the temple once more. At last it was finished, and everyone gave thanks to God.

Ezra 3-5

REBUILDING THE WALLS

The Samaritans tried to stop the Jews from rebuilding the city walls, but Nehemiah remained strong and told the people not to worry, for God was with them. Working with weapons by their sides, and from first light until the stars came out, they finished the walls in fifty-two days. The city was protected!

Then Nehemiah and the prophet Ezra gathered together the people. For two weeks Ezra taught the leaders more about God's law, and then the people gathered once more to make a solemn promise to God that they would obey his laws. At last they understood just how badly they had let him down. Now they planned to honor him and keep their side of the covenant.

Nehemiah 8-10

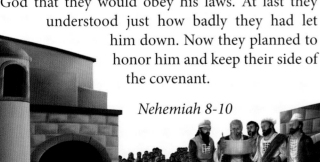

NEHEMIAH IN JERUSALEM

The temple may have been rebuilt, but the walls of Jerusalem still lay in ruins. When Nehemiah, a Jew in exile in Babylonia, learned of this, he got permission from the king to return to help rebuild the city.

When he arrived, he rode around the walls. In some places there was so much rubble that his donkey couldn't pass. The next morning he went to the leaders and said to them, "This is a disgrace! We need to rebuild the walls and make new gates. God answered my prayers when I wanted to come back, and he will help us now!" And so work began on the city walls.

Nehemiah 1-2

Map 14 C4

A MESSENGER IS COMING

Years had passed since the return to Jerusalem. To start with, everyone had been full of good intentions, but things had begun to slip. They didn't realize how much they had to be thankful for. God sent Malachi to them:

"You complain that God isn't blessing you. Yet you have stopped loving him with all your heart. Love and honor him, and then you will receive his full blessing.

"One day he will send a messenger to prepare the way. He will be like a blazing fire that burns away everything impure, leaving behind only those who will worship God properly. One day, God's judgment will come upon those who do wrong. But those of you who obey him will feel his power shine on you like the warm rays of the sun!"

The people of Israel now knew that one day a mighty messenger would come to prepare the way for the Lord!

Malachi 1-4

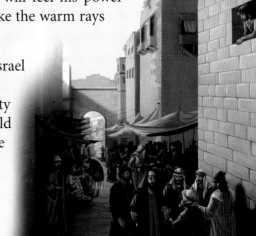

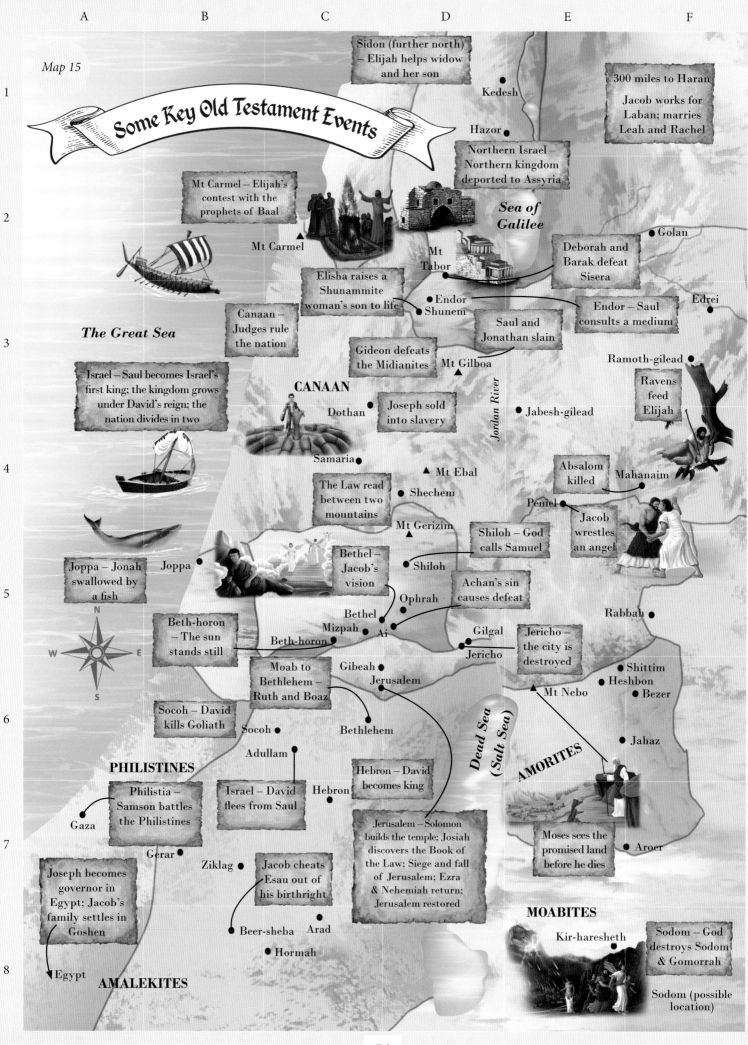

Map 15

Some Key Old Testament Events

A **B** **C** **D** **E** **F**

1

Sidon (further north) – Elijah helps widow and her son

Kedesh

Hazor

300 miles to Haran

Jacob works for Laban; marries Leah and Rachel

2

Mt Carmel – Elijah's contest with the prophets of Baal

Northern Israel – Northern kingdom deported to Assyria

Sea of Galilee

Mt Carmel

Golan

Mt Tabor

Deborah and Barak defeat Sisera

3

The Great Sea

Elisha raises a Shunammite woman's son to life

Endor
Shunem

Edrei

Canaan – Judges rule the nation

Endor – Saul consults a medium

Gideon defeats the Midianites

Saul and Jonathan slain

Mt Gilboa

Ramoth-gilead

Israel – Saul becomes Israel's first king; the kingdom grows under David's reign; the nation divides in two

CANAAN

Jordan River

Ravens feed Elijah

4

Dothan

Joseph sold into slavery

Jabesh-gilead

Samaria

Mt Ebal

Absalom killed

Mahanaim

The Law read between two mountains

Shechem

Peniel

Jacob wrestles an angel

Mt Gerizim

Shiloh – God calls Samuel

5

Joppa – Jonah swallowed by a fish

Joppa

Bethel – Jacob's vision

Shiloh

Ophrah

Achan's sin causes defeat

Beth-horon – The sun stands still

Bethel

Mizpah

Beth-horon

Ai

Gilgal

Jericho

Jericho – the city is destroyed

Rabbah

Gibeah

Shittim

Heshbon

Jerusalem

Bezer

Moab to Bethlehem – Ruth and Boaz

Mt Nebo

6

Socoh – David kills Goliath

Socoh

Bethlehem

Jahaz

Adullam

AMORITES

PHILISTINES

Hebron – David becomes king

Moses sees the promised land before he dies

Philistia – Samson battles the Philistines

Israel – David flees from Saul

Hebron

Dead Sea (Salt Sea)

Gaza

Aroer

7

Gerar

Jerusalem – Solomon builds the temple; Josiah discovers the Book of the Law; Siege and fall of Jerusalem; Ezra & Nehemiah return; Jerusalem restored

Joseph becomes governor in Egypt; Jacob's family settles in Goshen

Ziklag

Jacob cheats Esau out of his birthright

MOABITES

Beer-sheba

Arad

Kir-haresheth

Sodom – God destroys Sodom & Gomorrah

Egypt

Hormah

8

AMALEKITES

Sodom (possible location)

N W E S

56

GOD DESTROYS SODOM

In the time of Abraham, the people had turned away from God and had fallen back into wicked ways. There were two particularly evil cities—Sodom and Gomorrah. God promised Abraham that he would spare Sodom, where Abraham's nephew Lot had made his home, if there were as many as ten good people in the city. But when he sent angels to the city, only Lot and his family were found to be worthy.

The angels led Lot, his wife, and his two daughters to safety, warning them not to look back as the Lord rained fire and destruction on the wicked place. But Lot's wife could not resist looking behind her, and as she did so, she was turned into a pillar of salt. Only Lot and his two daughters escaped the devastation.

Genesis 18-19

Map 15
F8

THE PEACE TREATY

The walls of Jericho had fallen to the might of God, and the people of nearby Gibeon feared for their lives. They decided to trick the Israelites into signing a peace treaty with them, by pretending they came from a far-off land, and sent messengers dressed in ragged clothes, with stale bread and leaking waterskins to show how long they had been traveling.

Joshua was taken in by the trickery, and didn't stop to ask for God's advice. Instead, he drew up a peace treaty with the men of Gibeon on the spot and swore an oath to keep it.

When they learned the truth, the Israelites were furious, but they had sworn an oath in God's name and could not go back on their word.

Joshua 9-10

Map 15
D5

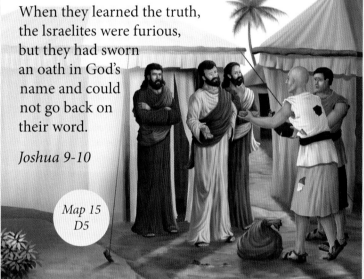

THE SUN AND THE MOON STAND STILL

Joshua and his army of Israelites had come to the aid of their allies, the people of Gibeon. They had marched through the night and caught their enemies by surprise. Throughout the battle, God was on their side. He sent great hailstones to fall on the enemy, and soon Joshua knew that the Israelites were winning—but he also knew night would fall before they could finish the battle!

Then Joshua called out, "Sun, stand still over Gibeon, and you, moon, over the Valley of Aijalon!" and God listened to Joshua and made the sun and the moon stand still until Joshua and his men had won the battle!

Joshua 10

Map 15
C5

DEBORAH AND JAEL

In the time of the judges, the Israelites came under attack from King Jabin of Hazor. A wise woman named Deborah told Barak, a soldier, to gather an army, for God had promised that Jabin's general and his soldiers would be delivered into his hands. Barak agreed to go, but only if Deborah went too!

The Israelites met General Sisera on the slopes of Mount Tabor and, with God's help, killed his entire army! But Sisera escaped and hid in the tent of one of the king's allies. There a woman named Jael gave him a drink and a place to rest, but as soon as he fell asleep, she killed him, for she secretly hated Sisera and his army!

When Barak came searching for Sisera, Jael told him what she had done. The Israelites praised her, while Deborah and Barak reminded them that it was God who had won the war for them.

Judges 4-5

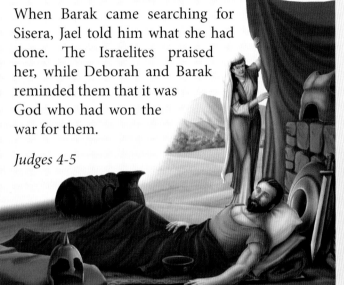

GIDEON AND THE THREE HUNDRED

Gideon was called by God to deliver the Israelites from the Midianites. Many thousands of men came to fight with him, but God said there were too many. He had Gideon send away all who were scared, and then he made him keep only those who drank from the river from their cupped hands. That left just three hundred men!

Gideon was afraid as he looked down upon the enemy camp, but God showed him that his enemy was just as scared as he was. That night Gideon gave all his men trumpets and empty jars with torches inside and led them down to the enemy camp. There they blew their trumpets, smashed the jars, and shouted out loud. The noise and sudden light startled the Midianites so much that the camp fell into confusion, and the soldiers fled in terror, turning on one another in their fright!

In this way, Gideon defeated the Midianites with just three hundred men! Everyone knew that the victory came from the power of God and not the power of men.

Judges 7

Map 15
D3

Map 15
C6

FAITHFUL RUTH

Naomi was moving back home to Bethlehem. Her husband and sons had died, and though she loved her two daughters-in-law dearly, she begged them to stay behind, for she knew her life would be hard. Orpah reluctantly agreed to go home to her mother, but loyal Ruth said, "Don't ask me to leave! I'll go wherever you go. Your people will be my people, and your God will be my God."

So Ruth and Naomi came to Bethlehem. Soon they had no food left, and Ruth went out into the fields and asked the owner if she could pick up any of the barley that his workers left behind during the harvest. The owner was Boaz. He kindly let Ruth work in his fields and told his servants to share their food with her. When Ruth returned with a basket of food, Naomi knew that God was looking after them, for Boaz was a relation of hers.

In time, Ruth married Boaz, and when they had a son, there was no happier woman in all of Bethlehem than Naomi!

Ruth 1-4

SAMSON, THE STRONGMAN

Samson was the strongest man alive. Since his birth his hair had never been cut—it was a sign that he belonged to God in a very special way. One day Samson was pounced upon by one of the fierce lions that roamed the land of Canaan. Samson was filled with the Spirit of the Lord, and he became so strong that he was able to kill the beast with his bare hands!

Samson was a thorn in the side of the Philistines, who had enslaved the Israelites for forty years. Although he never led an army, he carried out many attacks against them. But when he fell in love with Delilah, a beautiful Philistine woman, they bribed her to find out the secret of Samson's strength.

Night after night Delilah pleaded with Samson to tell her his secret. In the end, she wore him down, and he said, "If anyone were to cut my hair off, then I would lose all my strength." When Samson awoke, it was to discover that the Philistines had come into his room and cut off his hair. Now he was powerless as they bound and blinded him and threw him into prison!

Over time, Samson's hair grew back. One day, the Philistine rulers were all gathered for a feast in a crowded temple. Samson was brought out to be made fun of. He was chained between the two central pillars of the temple. Then Samson prayed to God with all his heart: "Give me strength just one more time, my Lord, so that I can take revenge upon my enemies!"

Once more Samson was filled with strength. He pushed against the pillars with all his might, and they toppled. The temple crashed down, killing everyone inside. Samson killed more of his enemies with this final act than he had killed in all of his life!

Judges 13-16

SAMUEL, THE PROPHET

Hannah longed to have a child, but to no avail. One year, when visiting the temple, she wept in sorrow and sent a silent prayer to God, 'Oh Lord, if you bless me with a child, I promise to give him back to you to serve for all his life!" When Eli the priest saw Hannah, he sent her on her way gently, saying, "May God answer your prayer."

Nine months later she gave birth to a baby boy and named him Samuel. When he was old enough, he went to serve Eli. One night Samuel awoke with a start when he heard his name called. He rushed to Eli's room,

but the priest sent him back to bed, saying, "I did not call you, child." But Samuel had barely pulled the covers back over him when he heard his name called again. As before, he rushed to the priest, but once more Eli sent him away. This happened one more time before Eli realized who was really calling Samuel—God! And so the next time Samuel heard a voice, he answered, and God spoke to him!

As Samuel grew up, God often spoke to him, and in time people listened to what Samuel had to say. He became a famous prophet and anointed the first king of Israel, Saul.

1 Samuel 1-3

ELIJAH AND THE RAVENS

Elijah was another of God's prophets, at the time when Israel was ruled by wicked King Ahab and his wife Jezebel. Elijah warned Ahab that God was angry and would send a drought to the land, and it happened as he said, but God sent Elijah east of the Jordan River to hide. There, ravens brought him bread and meat, and he drank from the brook.

1 Kings 17

Map 15
F3

ELIJAH AND THE WIDOW

When the brook dried up, God sent Elijah to Sidon, where a kind widow helped him even though she only had a handful of flour and a drop of oil left to make one last meal for herself and her son. Elijah told her to bake him a loaf of bread and promised that as long as the drought continued, the flour and oil would never ran out, and it happened as he said—there was always some flour and oil left for the next meal.

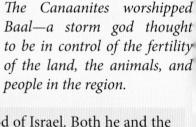

But one day the boy became ill, and then he stopped breathing. The widow was distraught, but Elijah took the boy up to his room, and there cried out to God.

Map 14
C4

God heard Elijah's cry, and the boy's life returned to him. The widow was filled with gratitude and awe and said, "Now I know that you are truly a man of God and that the word you preach is the truth!"

1 Kings 17

The Canaanites worshipped Baal—a storm god thought to be in control of the fertility of the land, the animals, and people in the region.

ELIJAH AND THE PRIESTS OF BAAL

For years there had been no rain, and there was famine throughout the land. Elijah persuaded King Ahab to gather the people of Israel and the prophets of Baal at Mount Carmel, and he proposed a test so that they could learn who was the true God of Israel. Both he and the prophets of Baal would prepare a bull for sacrifice. Then each would call upon their god to answer with fire!

The many priests of Baal prepared their bull and then called upon their god to send fire. They prayed and tore their clothes, but nothing happened. "Perhaps Baal hasn't heard you," mocked Elijah. "Try harder!" But try as they might, there was no answer, and at last they fell to the ground in exhaustion.

Now Elijah used twelve stones to build an altar, around which he dug a trench. He prepared the bull and laid it on the wood. Then he got the people to soak the sacrifice and wood with water until it filled the trench. He prayed to God before the people, and the fire of the Lord burned up the sacrifice, the wood, the stones, and even the water!

The people fell to their knees. "The Lord is God!" they cried. Elijah made sure that the prophets of Baal were seized and slain, and by evening the rains came and the famine was ended.

1 Kings 18

Map 15
C2

ELISHA CARRIES ON THE TRADITION

When Elijah died, his disciple Elisha inherited his spirit and carried on his work. Once, a woman who had been kind to him was sad because she had no children. Elisha promised her that within a year she would have a son, and it happened just as he said.

But one day, the young boy became ill and died in his mother's arms. The woman left the boy lying on his bed as if sleeping, spoke to no one, and then went to Elisha. Filled with anguish, she reproached him for ever having asked God to give her a son.

Elisha traveled with her back to her home, went into the boy's room alone, and prayed to God. He lay beside the boy to warm his body, paced round the room, and then warmed him again.

Suddenly the boy sneezed! He sneezed seven times and then opened his eyes!

Elisha called the woman in, and she took her son in her arms! Her gratitude toward Elisha and God was immeasurable.

Judges 7

Map 15
D3

JONAH AND THE BIG FISH

Jonah was a prophet, but when God sent him to Ninevah to tell the people there that he would destroy their city if they didn't mend their ways, Jonah didn't want to go. The people of Ninevah were enemies of the Jews, and he felt that they deserved to be punished. So instead, he boarded a ship in Joppa heading in the opposite direction.

Map 15
B5

But soon a dreadful storm sprang up from nowhere. Certain that they would drown, the sailors drew straws to see which of them had angered the gods. When Jonah picked the short straw, he had to tell them that he was running away from God. He realized how wicked he had been and insisted that the sailors throw him overboard—and as soon as they did, the storm ended.

Jonah sank below the waves but was swallowed whole by an enormous fish. He spent three days and nights inside the belly of the fish. He had plenty of time to think about his mistakes and to feel very sorry for having disobeyed

God. He prayed to God, thanking him for delivering him from the sea and letting him know how remorseful he felt.

After three days, God commanded the fish to spit Jonah up unharmed onto dry land. And when God once again asked him to take his message to Nineveh, Jonah was ready to do his will.

Jonah 1-2

In many ways, the story of Jonah and the whale prefigures the life of Jesus. In particular, the fact that Jonah emerges from the whale after three days foreshadows the resurrection, for Jesus rose on the third day.

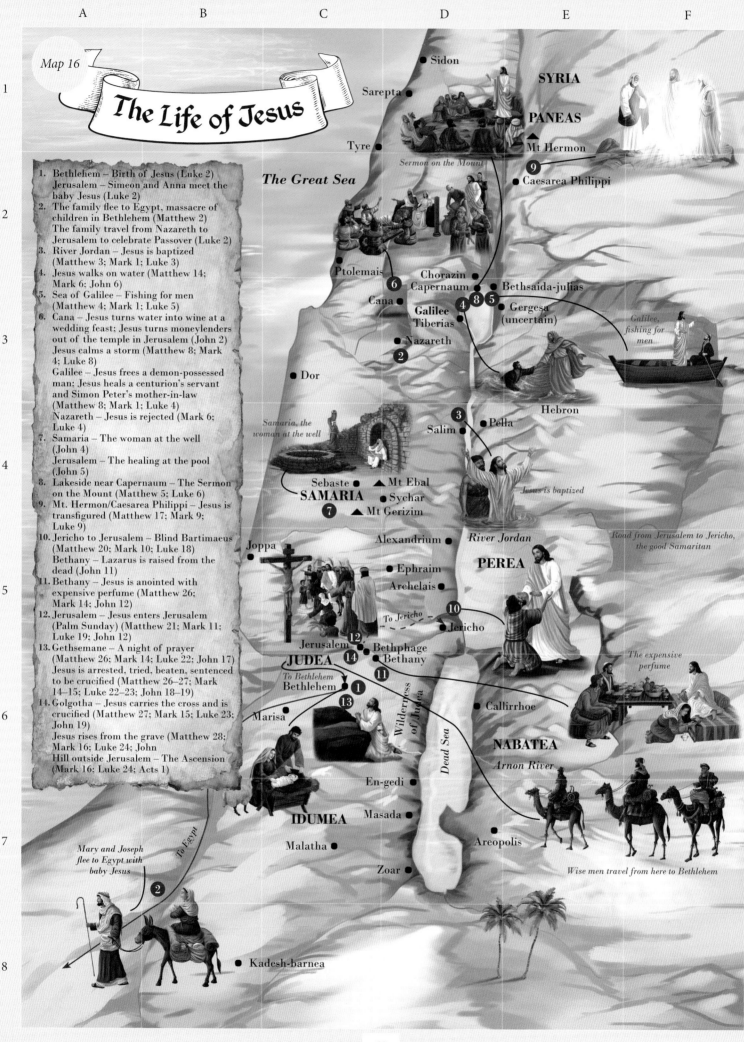

Map 16

The Life of Jesus

1. Bethlehem – Birth of Jesus (Luke 2)
   Jerusalem – Simeon and Anna meet the baby Jesus (Luke 2)
2. The family flee to Egypt, massacre of children in Bethlehem (Matthew 2)
   The family travel from Nazareth to Jerusalem to celebrate Passover (Luke 2)
3. River Jordan – Jesus is baptized (Matthew 3; Mark 1; Luke 3)
4. Jesus walks on water (Matthew 14; Mark 6; John 6)
5. Sea of Galilee – Fishing for men (Matthew 4; Mark 1; Luke 5)
6. Cana – Jesus turns water into wine at a wedding feast; Jesus turns moneylenders out of the temple in Jerusalem (John 2)
   Jesus calms a storm (Matthew 8; Mark 4; Luke 8)
   Galilee – Jesus frees a demon-possessed man; Jesus heals a centurion's servant and Simon Peter's mother-in-law (Matthew 8; Mark 1; Luke 4)
   Nazareth – Jesus is rejected (Mark 6; Luke 4)
7. Samaria – The woman at the well (John 4)
   Jerusalem – The healing at the pool (John 5)
8. Lakeside near Capernaum – The Sermon on the Mount (Matthew 5; Luke 6)
9. Mt. Hermon/Caesarea Philippi – Jesus is transfigured (Matthew 17; Mark 9; Luke 9)
10. Jericho to Jerusalem – Blind Bartimaeus (Matthew 20; Mark 10; Luke 18)
    Bethany – Lazarus is raised from the dead (John 11)
11. Bethany – Jesus is anointed with expensive perfume (Matthew 26; Mark 14; John 12)
12. Jerusalem – Jesus enters Jerusalem (Palm Sunday) (Matthew 21; Mark 11; Luke 19; John 12)
13. Gethsemane – A night of prayer (Matthew 26; Mark 14; Luke 22; John 17)
    Jesus is arrested, tried, beaten, sentenced to be crucified (Matthew 26–27; Mark 14–15; Luke 22–23; John 18–19)
14. Golgotha – Jesus carries the cross and is crucified (Matthew 27; Mark 15; Luke 23; John 19)
    Jesus rises from the grave (Matthew 28; Mark 16; Luke 24; John)
    Hill outside Jerusalem – The Ascension (Mark 16; Luke 24; Acts 1)

A B C D E F

1
2
3
4
5
6
7
8

Sidon
Sarepta
Tyre

SYRIA
PANEAS
Mt Hermon

Sermon on the Mount

The Great Sea

Caesarea Philippi

9

Ptolemais
Cana
Chorazin
Capernaum
Galilee
Tiberias
Nazareth
Bethsaida-julias
Gergesa (uncertain)

6
4 **8** **5**
2

Galilee, fishing for men

Dor

Hebron

Samaria, the woman at the well

Salim
Pella

3

Sebaste
Mt Ebal
Sychar

SAMARIA

7
Mt Gerizim

Jesus is baptized

Joppa

Alexandrium
River Jordan

Road from Jerusalem to Jericho, the good Samaritan

Ephraim
Archelais

PEREA

To Jericho
Jericho

10

Jerusalem
Bethphage
Bethany

12

JUDEA

14
11

The expensive perfume

To Bethlehem
Bethlehem

1

13

Marisa

Wilderness of Judea

Callirrhoe

Dead Sea

NABATEA

Arnon River

En-gedi

IDUMEA
Masada

Malatha

Areopolis

To Egypt

Mary and Joseph flee to Egypt with baby Jesus

2

Zoar

Wise men travel from here to Bethlehem

Kadesh-barnea

MARY IS CHOSEN BY GOD

Mary lived in Nazareth in Galilee and was engaged to Joseph, a carpenter who could trace his family back to King David. One day she was visited by the angel Gabriel, for God had chosen her for a very special honor: "You will give birth to a son and are to call him Jesus. He will be called the Son of God, and his kingdom will never end!"

Filled with wonder, Mary asked, "How can this be? I'm not even married!"

"Everything is possible for God," replied the angel. "The Holy Spirit will come on you, and your child will be God's own Son."

Mary bowed her head humbly, saying, "It will be as God wills it."

Luke 1

*Map 16
D3*

JESUS IS BORN

At this time, the emperor of Rome ordered a census. The Roman empire was at the height of its power and covered a vast area, and the emperor wanted to make sure he kept tabs on every single one of his subjects. All the people throughout the lands ruled by Rome had to go to their hometown to be counted.

Mary and Joseph had to travel to Bethlehem. By the time they arrived, the town was crowded. Every inn was full, and they spent the night in a stable, where Mary gave birth to her baby. She named him Jesus and laid him in a manger to sleep.

Shepherds in the hills above Bethlehem were visited by an angel of the Lord. He sent them to Bethlehem to see the new Savior, the Messiah, who had been born that night. The shepherds rushed to Bethlehem, where they found Jesus and knelt before him in wonder. They couldn't wait to tell everyone about this special baby and the wonderful news!

Luke 2

*Map 16
C6*

THE BRIGHT STAR

In a distant land far to the east, wise men had been studying the stars. When a really bright star was discovered, they followed it all the way to Judea, for they believed it was a sign that a great king had been born. When King Herod found out that they were looking for the future king of the Jews, he asked them to visit him on their return, to tell him where the baby was.

The wise men followed the star to Bethlehem, where they found baby Jesus in a humble house. They knelt before him and presented gifts of gold, frankincense, and myrrh before returning home. But they did not stop off at Herod's palace, for God had warned them in a dream not to go there.

When angry Herod then ordered his soldiers to search for the baby themselves and kill him, an angel warned Joseph. He took Mary and Jesus to Egypt, where they stayed until it was safe to return to Nazareth, where Jesus grew up.

Matthew 2

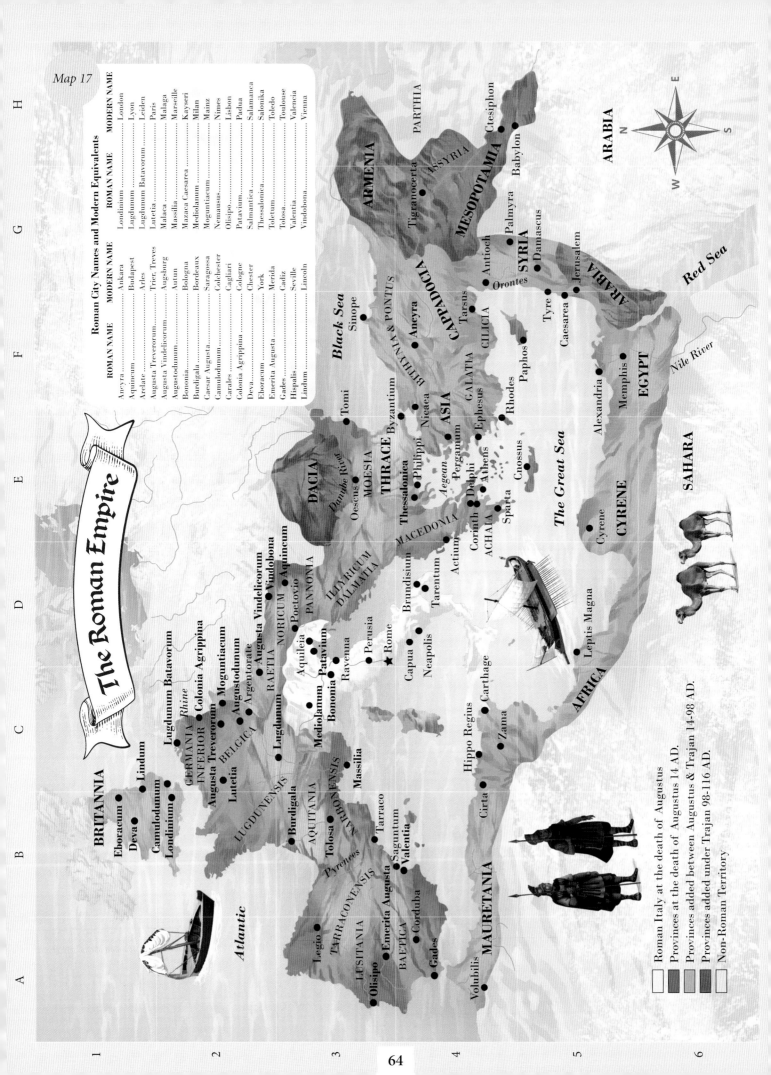

Map 17

The Roman Empire

Roman City Names and Modern Equivalents

ROMAN NAME	MODERN NAME	ROMAN NAME	MODERN NAME
Ancyra	Ankara	Londinium	London
Aquincum	Budapest	Lugdunum	Lyon
Arelate	Arles	Lugdunum Batavorum	Leiden
Augusta Treverorum	Trier, Treves	Lutetia	Paris
Augusta Vindelicorum	Augsburg	Malaca	Malaga
Augustodunum	Autun	Massilia	Marseille
Bononia	Bologna	Mazaca Caesarea	Kayseri
Burdigala	Bordeaux	Mediolanum	Milan
Caesar Augusta	Saragossa	Moguntiacum	Mainz
Camulodunum	Colchester	Nemausus	Nimes
Carales	Cagliari	Olisipo	Lisbon
Colonia Agrippina	Cologne	Patavium	Padua
Deva	Chester	Salmantica	Salamanca
Eboracum	York	Thessalonica	Salonika
Emerita Augusta	Merida	Toletum	Toledo
Gades	Cadiz	Tolosa	Toulouse
Hispalis	Seville	Valentia	Valencia
Lindum	Lincoln	Vindobona	Vienna

Legend:

- Roman Italy at the death of Augustus
- Provinces at the death of Augustus 14 AD.
- Provinces added between Augustus & Trajan 14-98 AD.
- Provinces added under Trajan 98-116 AD.
- Non-Roman Territory

JESUS IS BAPTIZED

Jesus' cousin, John, was living in the desert when God called him. He wore clothes made of camels' hair and lived on locusts and wild honey. God wanted John to prepare the people for the coming of his Son, so John traveled throughout the land preaching to people. He explained that they needed to repent and to change their ways. Many were truly sorry, and John baptized them in the river Jordan, as a sign that their sins had been washed away and they could start afresh.

At that time, Jesus came from Nazareth to the river Jordan where John was preaching. John knew at once that this was the promised King, the Lamb of God. So when Jesus asked him to baptize him, John was shocked and said, "*I should be asking you to baptize me!*" But Jesus insisted.

Just as Jesus was coming up from the water, the heavens opened, the Spirit descended on him like a dove, and a voice came from heaven, "You are my Son, whom I love; with you I am well pleased."

Map 16 D4

Matthew 3; Mark 1; Luke 3

TESTED IN THE DESERT

Map 16 D3

Jesus spent forty days and nights in the dry, hot desert as a test. He ate nothing. The devil came to him and said, "If you are the Son of God, why don't you tell these stones to become bread?"

Jesus answered calmly, "It is written: 'Man shall not live on bread alone, but on every word that comes from the mouth of God.'" Jesus knew that food wasn't the most important thing.

The devil took Jesus to the top of a temple and told him to throw himself off, for surely angels would rescue him. Jesus said, "It is also written: 'Do not put the Lord your God to the test.'"

From a high mountain, the devil offered him all the kingdoms of the world if Jesus would bow down and worship him. But Jesus replied, "Away from me, Satan! For it is written: 'Worship the Lord your God, and serve him alone.'"

When the devil realized that he could not tempt Jesus, he gave up and left him, and God sent his angels to Jesus to help him to recover.

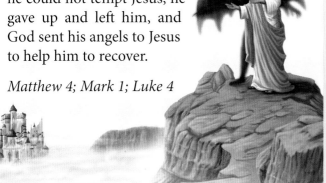

Matthew 4; Mark 1; Luke 4

FISHING FOR MEN

Jesus returned to Galilee and began to preach. Word soon spread, and people traveled to hear him. One day, on the shore of Lake Galilee, the crowd was so large that Jesus asked a fisherman if he would take him out in his boat a little way so everyone could see him.

Afterward, Jesus told Simon, the fisherman, to take the boat out farther and let down his nets. "Master," Simon answered, "we were out all night and caught nothing. But if you say so, then we will try again."

He couldn't believe his eyes when he pulled up his nets full of fish! He called to his brother, Andrew, and to his friends James and John to help, and soon the two boats were so full of fish that they were ready to sink!

Simon fell to his knees, but Jesus smiled. "Don't be afraid, Simon. From now on you shall be called Peter,* for that is what you will be." Then he turned to all the men. "Leave your nets," he said, "and come with me, and fish for men instead, so that we can spread the good news!" The men pulled the boats up on the beach, left everything, and followed Jesus.

Matthew 4; Mark 1; Luke 5

* *In Greek, "petra" means rock.*

Map 16 D3

WATER INTO WINE

Jesus was invited to a wedding party in Cana along with his friends and his mother. Everything was going well until the wine ran out. Mary came to tell Jesus, who asked her, "Why are you telling me this? It is not yet time for me to show myself." But Mary still hoped he would help and spoke quietly to the servants, telling them to do whatever Jesus told them to.

There were several huge water jars nearby. Jesus told the servants to fill them with water and then pour the water into jugs and take it to the head waiter to taste. When the head waiter tasted it, he exclaimed to the bridegroom, "Most people serve the best wine at the start of a meal, but you have saved the best till last!" for the jugs were now filled with delicious wine.

This was the first of many miracles that Jesus would perform.

John 2

Map 16
D3

HEALING

One time, a man with an awful skin disease came up to Jesus and fell to his knees on the ground. "Sir, if you want to, you can make me clean," he begged humbly.

Filled with compassion, Jesus reached out to touch the man. "I do want to," he said. "Be clean!" Immediately the man's skin was perfectly smooth and healthy!

The grateful man simply couldn't keep the wonderful event to himself, and before long so many people wanted to come and see Jesus that he could no longer go anywhere without being surrounded by crowds—people who were sick or lame or blind or crippled, and others who were troubled by evil spirits. Many would bring their friends or loved ones to see if this amazing man could help them too. And Jesus would lay his hands on each one and heal them.

Matthew 8; Mark 1; Luke 4-5

THE SERMON ON THE MOUNT

Jesus wasn't always welcome in the synagogues, so he would often teach his disciples and the large crowds that gathered to hear him outside in the open air. One of the most important talks he gave was on a mountain near Capernaum. It has become known as the Sermon on the Mount. Jesus taught the people about what was truly important in life and gave comfort and advice:

"How happy are the poor and those who are sad or who have been badly treated, those who are humble, gentle, and kind, and those who try to do the right thing—for all these people will be rewarded in heaven! They will be comforted and know great joy. Those who have been merciful will receive mercy, and God will look kindly on those who have tried to keep the peace, for they are truly his children. So be glad when people are mean to you and say nasty things about you because of me—for a great reward is waiting for you in heaven!"

Matthew 5; Luke 6

WISE WORDS

Jesus was not like their usual teachers. He told them, "It is important to obey all of God's laws, but you need to understand the meaning behind them. You must learn to forgive to become close to God. So instead of thinking, 'An eye for an eye, and a tooth for a tooth,' if someone slaps you on the cheek, offer him the other one too! Anger will eat you up. It's easy to love those who love you, but I say, love your enemies!

"Let your life be an example to others, but don't do good things just so people will look at you and think how good you are. Do your good deeds in private, and God, who sees everything, will reward you. And treat others in the same way that you would like them to treat you. Don't judge them. Think about your own faults first!"

He told people how to pray. "Keep on asking," said Jesus, "and you will receive. Keep on seeking, and you will find. Keep on knocking, and the door will be opened."

Matthew 5-7; Luke 6; 11

CHOOSING THE TWELVE

Jesus chose twelve men to be his special disciples: Simon Peter and his brother Andrew, and brothers James and John, were all fishermen; Matthew (or Levi) was a tax collector; Simon was a patriot who wanted to fight the Romans; and the other six were Bartholomew, Thomas, James son of Alphaeus, Philip, Judas (or Thaddeus) son of James, and Judas Iscariot.

Jesus knew they would have a hard task ahead of them. He wanted them to teach the people that God's kingdom is near and to heal people too. He sent them out to travel from village to village, taking nothing with them except for a staff because God would provide everything they needed. Everywhere they went they were to rely on the hospitality of the people, and if they were not made welcome, then they were to leave. But those who welcomed them were really welcoming Jesus himself.

Matthew 10; Mark 3; 6

CALMING THE STORM

Jesus and his disciples climbed into a boat to travel across to the other side of the lake. Jesus was so tired that he lay down and fell asleep. Suddenly, the skies darkened, rain came pelting down, and a fierce storm struck the lake. Huge waves tossed the boat, and the disciples were terrified that they would capsize.

Jesus still lay sleeping. The frightened disciples went over and woke him, begging him to save them. Jesus opened his eyes and looked up at them. "Why are you afraid? You have so little faith!" he said sadly. Then he stood up calmly, his arms spread wide, and facing into the wind and rain, commanded, "Be still!" At once the wind and waves died down, and all was calm.

The disciples were amazed. "Who is this man?" they asked themselves. "Even the winds and waves obey him!"

Matthew 8; Mark 4;
Luke 8

Map 16
D3

THE WOMAN AT THE WELL

Passing through Samaria, Jesus stopped at a well and asked a local woman for a drink. She was taken aback, because normally Jews wouldn't talk to Samaritans. She was even more surprised when he said, "If you knew what God can give you and who it is that asks for a drink, you would have asked and he would have given you living water."

When she asked where he could get such water, Jesus replied, "Those who drink this water will get thirsty again, but those who drink the water I will give them will never be thirsty again."

The woman asked eagerly for the water, but when Jesus told her to fetch her husband, she blushed and said she didn't have one. When Jesus replied that she had had five husbands and wasn't married to the one she was living with, she said he must be a prophet, and he explained that he was the Messiah.

She told her friends about the amazing man, and many went to see him for themselves and believed because of that day.

John 4

Map 16
C4

THE OFFICER'S SERVANT

In Capernaum there lived a Roman officer who was a good man. One of his servants was sick and close to death. When the officer heard that Jesus had come to Capernaum, he came to ask for his help, and Jesus asked him if he should come to his house to heal the servant.

The officer replied, "Lord, I do not deserve to have you come to my own house, but I know that you don't need to. If you just say the word, I know that my servant will be healed, in the same way that when I order my soldiers to do something, they do it!"

Jesus said to the crowd following him, "I tell you all, I have never found faith like this, even in Israel!"

When the officer returned to his house, he found his servant up on his feet and feeling perfectly well again!

Matthew 8; Luke 7

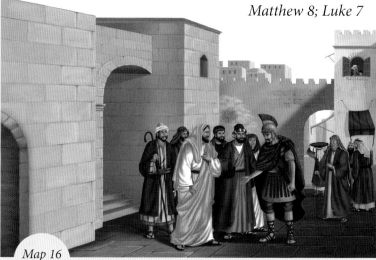

Map 16
D3

FEEDING FIVE THOUSAND

Jesus had been preaching to a huge crowd of people. When evening came, they didn't leave, for they all wanted to hear everything that Jesus had to say. Jesus told his disciples to give them something to eat.

"But Master," the disciples said, "there are thousands of people, and we only have five loaves of bread and two fish!"

Jesus commanded them to tell the people to sit down. Then, taking the five loaves and the two fish and looking up to heaven, he gave thanks to his Father and broke the loaves into pieces. He gave them to the disciples, who took them to the people and then came back to Jesus for more bread and fish. He filled up their baskets again . . . and again . . . and again! To their astonishment there was still bread and fish left in the baskets when they came to feed the very last people! More than five thousand people had been fed that day—with five loaves of bread and two fish!

Matthew 14; Mark 6; Luke 9; John 6

PARABLE OF THE SOWER

Jesus tried to pass on his message in a way that people would understand. His stories, often called parables, let people think things through for themselves. To some they would just be stories, but others would understand the real message.

"A farmer went out to sow his seed. As he was scattering it, some fell along the path and was trampled on or eaten by birds. Some fell on rocky ground where there was no soil, and when they began to grow, the plants withered because their roots could not reach water. Other seeds fell among weeds that choked them. Still others fell on good soil and grew into tall, strong plants and produced a crop far greater than what was sown."

Jesus was telling them that he was like the farmer, and the seeds were like the message he brought from God. The seeds that fell on the path and were eaten are like people who hear but pay no attention. Those on rocky ground are like those who receive the word with joy and believe for a while, but when life gets difficult they give up. The seeds among weeds are like those who hear but let themselves become choked by life's worries. But the seeds that fell on good soil are like those who hear God's message and hold it tight in their heart. Their faith grows and grows.

Matthew 13; Mark 4; Luke 8

THE GOOD SAMARITAN

Once someone asked Jesus what the Law meant when it said we must love our neighbors as much as ourselves. "Who is my neighbor?" he asked. Jesus told him a story:

"A man was going from Jerusalem to Jericho when he was attacked by robbers who beat him and took everything before leaving him by the roadside, half dead. Soon a priest passed by. He saw the man but crossed to the other side of the road and continued on his way. Then a Levite came along. He also hurried on his way without stopping.

"Then a Samaritan came along. He knelt beside the man and carefully washed and bandaged his wounds. He took him on his donkey to an inn, where he gave the innkeeper money to look after the man until he was well."

Jesus looked at the man who had posed the question and asked who he thought had been a good neighbor to the injured man.

The man sheepishly replied, "The one who was kind to him."

Then Jesus told him, "Go, then, and be like him."

Luke 10

THE LOST SON

Jesus told a story to explain how happy God was when sinners returned to him: "There was once a man with two sons. The younger one asked for his share of the property, left home, and soon spent it all on enjoying himself. He ended up working for a farmer and was so hungry that he wanted to eat the food he was giving to the pigs! At last he set off for home to tell his father how sorry he was. 'I'm not worthy of being his son,' he thought, 'but maybe he will let me work on the farm.'

"When his father saw him coming, he rushed out and hugged him. The young man tried to tell him that he was not fit to be called his son, but the father told his servants to prepare a feast.

"The older son was outraged. Nobody had ever held a feast for him and he had worked hard for his father. 'My son,' his father said, 'you are always with me, and all I have is yours. But celebrate with me now, for your brother was dead to me and is alive again; he was lost and is found!'"

Luke 15

WALKING ON WATER

It was late at night, and waves tossed the boat violently. Jesus had stayed ashore to pray, and the disciples were afraid. At the first light of dawn, they saw a figure walking toward them on the water! They thought it was a ghost and were scared until they heard the calm voice of Jesus: "It is I. Don't be afraid."

"Lord," said Simon Peter, "if it is you, command me to walk across the water to you," and Jesus did so.

Simon Peter put one foot gingerly in the water. Then he lowered the other and stood up. He didn't sink! But when he looked around, his courage failed him. As he began to sink, he cried, "Lord, save me!"

Jesus reached out and took his hand. "Oh, Peter," he said sadly, "where is your faith? Why did you doubt?" Then together they walked back to the boat. The wind died down, and the water became calm. The disciples bowed low. "Truly you are the Son of God," they said humbly.

Matthew 14; Mark 6; John 6

Map 16
D3

MARTHA AND MARY

Jesus was fond of two sisters—Mary and Martha. One day, Jesus stopped to visit. Martha rushed off to make sure everything was clean and tidy and to prepare food, but Mary sat by his feet, listening to everything he said, not wanting to miss a single word.

Martha was angry. "Lord," she said to Jesus, "won't you tell Mary to help me? There is so much to get ready, and she is sitting there doing nothing while I do all the work!"

"Martha," said Jesus in a soothing voice, "you are worrying about small things, but they are not what is really important. Your sister understands what is truly important, and it will not be taken away from her." He was trying to explain that the most important thing in life is to love Jesus and listen to his words!

Luke 10

Map 16
C6

LAZARUS LIVES!

Jesus received a message from Martha and Mary, telling him that their brother, Lazarus, was very ill. By the time Jesus arrived at their house, Lazarus was dead. Martha wept, saying, "Oh Lord, if you had been here, my brother would not have died. But I know that God will give you whatever you ask."

Then Jesus said gently, "He will rise again. Everyone who believes in me will live again, even though he has died." But when Mary came up weeping, and he saw the other relatives crying, then Jesus wept too, and asked to be taken to the cave where Lazarus had been laid. Though Lazarus had been dead for four days, Jesus told the men to open it. He and gave thanks to God. Then he commanded, "Lazarus, come out!"

Everyone watched in silent wonder as a figure emerged from the dark cave, his hands and feet wrapped with strips of linen, and a cloth around his face. It was Lazarus, and he was alive!

John 11

THE TRANSFIGURATION

Jesus climbed up a mountain to pray, taking with him Peter, James, and John. All of a sudden, as Jesus prayed, the disciples looked up to see him changed. Light shone from his face and clothes, and as they watched in wonder, Moses, who had led his people out of Egypt, and Elijah, greatest of all the prophets, were suddenly there before their very eyes, talking with Jesus! Then a bright cloud covered them, and a voice said, "This is my Son, whom I love. Listen to what he has to say, for I am very pleased with him!"

The disciples fell to the ground, too frightened to raise their eyes. But Jesus came over and touched them. "Don't be afraid," he said softly, and when they looked up, they saw no one there except Jesus.

Matthew 17; Mark 9; Luke 9

*Map 16
E2*

BLIND BARTIMAEUS

Jesus was passing through Jericho on his way to Jerusalem. Blind Bartimaeus was begging by the roadside when he heard a great commotion around him. When he learned that it was Jesus of Nazareth, of whom he had heard so many wonderful things, he struggled to his feet and called out, "Jesus, Son of David, have mercy on me!"

People shushed him, but he kept calling. Jesus heard him and stopped by the roadside. "What do you want me to do for you?" he asked gently.

Bartimaeus fell to his knees. "Lord, I want to see!" he begged.

"Receive your sight," said Jesus. "Your faith has healed you." Immediately Bartimaeus' eyes were cleared and he could see everything around him! Instantly, he jumped up and followed Jesus, praising God. When all the people saw him, they praised God too!

Matthew 20; Mark 10; Luke 18

*Map 16
D5*

THE EXPENSIVE PERFUME

One evening, shortly before Passover, Jesus was dining with his disciples and friends in Bethany. Mary came to him, carrying an expensive jar of perfume. Kneeling before him, she carefully poured the perfume on his feet, using her own hair to wipe them. The house was filled with the wonderful fragrance.

Some started to scold her, for the perfume could have been sold to raise money for the poor. Jesus hushed them. "She has done a beautiful thing," he said. "You will always have the poor, and you can help them any time you want. But you won't always have me. People will remember Mary's kindness to me."

For Jesus would not be with them in this way for much longer. The final stage of his time on earth was about to begin.

Matthew 26; Mark 14; John 12

*Map 16
C6*

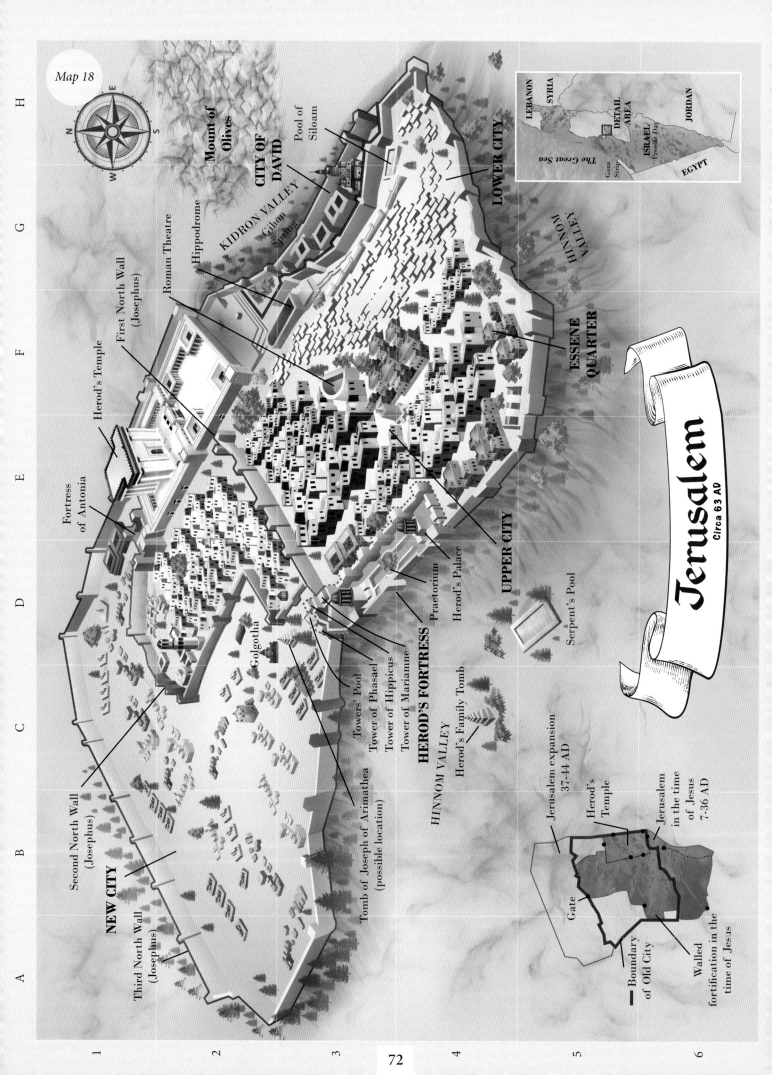

Map 18

N E S W

Jerusalem
Circa 63 AD

LEBANON
SYRIA
DETAIL AREA
ISRAEL Present Day
JORDAN
The Great Sea
Gaza Strip
EGYPT

Mount of Olives

CITY OF DAVID

Pool of Siloam

KIDRON VALLEY

Gihon Spring

Hippodrome

Roman Theatre

First North Wall (Josephus)

Herod's Temple

Fortress of Antonia

Second North Wall (Josephus)

NEW CITY

Third North Wall (Josephus)

LOWER CITY

HINNOM VALLEY

ESSENE QUARTER

UPPER CITY

Golgotha

Tomb of Joseph of Arimathea (possible location)

Towers' Pool

Tower of Phasael

Tower of Hippicus

Tower of Marianne

HEROD'S FORTRESS

Praetorium

Herod's Palace

HINNOM VALLEY

Herod's Family Tomb

Serpent's Pool

Jerusalem expansion 37-44 AD

Herod's Temple

Jerusalem in the time of Jesus 7-36 AD

Gate

Boundary of Old City

Walled fortification in the time of Jesus

72

Jesus' Last Week

Jerusalem was packed. It was the week of the Passover festival, and everyone had gathered to celebrate. It was also time for Jesus to start the last stage of his earthly life.

Jesus entered Jerusalem riding a humble donkey. Some of his followers threw their cloaks or large palm leaves on the dusty ground before him, and he was met by an enormous crowd, for many had heard of the miracles he had performed. Some of the religious leaders feared and hated Jesus, but many of the people truly saw him as their King, and they tried to give him a king's welcome.

His followers cried out, "Hosanna to the Son of David! Blessed is the king who comes in the name of the Lord!"

But Jesus was sad, for he knew that in a very short time these people cheering him would turn against him.

Matthew 21; Mark 11; Luke 19; John 12

TROUBLE IN THE TEMPLE

The first thing Jesus did in Jerusalem was to visit his Father's temple. He was appalled to find that all the greedy, cheating people that he had thrown out before were back again, trying to make money out of the poor people who came to make sacrifices to God. He looked around in anger, shouting, "No! God said that this temple was to be a place where people from all nations could come to pray to him. But you have made it a den of robbers!" And with these words he tore through the temple, throwing everyone out who shouldn't be there.

When he had finished and the temple was once again calm and tranquil, the poor people, the beggars, and the sick began to find their way back in and came to Jesus to be healed and to feel better. Children danced for joy around him, and everyone was happy—apart from the Pharisees, who plotted to get rid of him.

Matthew 21; Mark 11; Luke 19

Map 18
E1-2

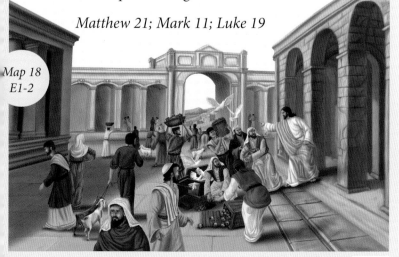

BETRAYAL

Jesus knew that the Pharisees and those who hated and feared him were waiting for any opportunity to arrest him. He spent the days in Jerusalem in the temple, but each night he returned to Bethany to sleep. Yet even among his dearest friends there was one who would be his enemy.

Judas Iscariot, the disciple in charge of the money, was dishonest. He kept some for himself instead of giving it to those who needed it. His greed made him do a very bad thing. Judas went to the chief priests in secret and asked them how much they would give him if he delivered Jesus into their hands.

The priests couldn't believe their ears! They knew Judas was one of Jesus' most trusted friends. They offered him thirty pieces of silver . . . and Judas accepted! From then on, Judas was simply waiting for the opportunity to hand Jesus over.

Matthew 26; Mark 14; Luke 22

73

Map 19

Golgotha ●
(Gordon's Calvary)

Second North Wall (Josephus)

Fish Gate

Fort Antonia

29
31

Sheep Pool

Temple Pool

Sheep Gate

Tyropoeon Valley

Golgotha
(traditional location)

32

First North Wall

Aystus

Josephus

Towers' Pool

Tower of Hippicus

Tower of Phasael

Gennath Gate

Tower of Mariamne

Herod's Palace

30

House of Caiaphas,
the High Priest

JERUSALEM

UPPER CITY

27

26

Serpent's Pool

22

LOWER CITY

TYROPOEON VALLEY

City of David

Siloam Pool

Essene Gate

HINNOM VALLEY

The Outer Court

28
20

Temple

18 **15**

14

13

12

Inner Court

11

4 **7** **8** **10**

Kidron Valley

OPHEL

Citadel

Gihon Spring

Herekiah's Tunnel

Water Gate

3 **6** **9** **16** **17**

Mount of Olives **23**

25 **24**

Gethsemane

Garden of Gethsemane

Bethphage

2

Jesus' Last Week

1 **5**
Bethany

19 **21**

Sunday
1. Jesus leaves Bethany.
2. His disciples go ahead to the village of Bethphage to fetch a donkey.
3. Jesus rides over the Mount of Olives and into the city crossing the Kidron Valley. The crowd cheers, and waves palm branches in the air, as Jesus weeps for the city of Jerusalem (Luke 19:41).
4. Jesus enters Jerusalem and visits the temple, before returning to Bethany in the evening (Mark 11:11).

Monday
5. Jesus leaves Bethany.
6. On his way into Jerusalem he curses a fig tree on the Mount of Olives (Mark 11.12-14).
7. When he arrives in the temple, Jesus drives out all the buyers and sellers. (Matthew 21:12; Mark 11:15; Luke 19:45)
8. Jesus is visited by Greeks (John 12:20) and leaves the city in the evening (Mark 11:19) and returns to Bethany.

Tuesday
9. The disciples notice that the tree that Jesus had cursed on Monday has withered (Mark 11:20).
10. Jesus leaves Bethany and goes to the temple, where priests ask him about his behaviour from the day before (Matthew 21:23; Mark 11:27; Luke 20:1).
11. Jesus tells the Parable of the Two Sons (Matthew 21:28), the Parable of the Tenants (Matthew 21:33), and the Parable of the Wedding Banquet (Matthew 22:1).
12. Pharisees and Herodians try to trap him with a tax question (Matthew 22:15), the Sadducees ask him about the resurrection (Matthew 22:23), and Pharisees question him about the commandments (Matthew 22:34). Jesus asks them all: "Whose son is the Christ" (Matthew 22:41).
13. Jesus pronounces seven woes on the religious leaders (Matthew 23).
14. Jesus watches the widow give her only two coins (Mark 12:41; Luke 21:1-4).
15. Jesus' disciples show him the stones as he is leaving the temple. He tells them that the temple will be destroyed (Matthew 24:1-2).

16. Jesus talks to his disciples about the destruction of the temple, his return and The End on the Mount of Olives (Matthew 23-24; Mark 11; Luke 20-21).

Wednesday
17. Jesus tells his disciples that the Passover is two days away and that the Son of Man will be crucified (Matthew 26:1).
18. The chief priest and elders try to find a way to have Jesus killed (Matthew 26:2-5; Mark 14:1-2).
19. Jesus eats at the house of Simon the Leper and is anointed for the second time while he is in Bethany. His disciples complain about the waste of the expensive oil (Matthew 26:6-13; Mark 14:3-9).
20. Judas goes to the chief priests to plan his betrayal (Matthew 26:14-16; Mark 14:10-11; Luke 22:3-6).

Thursday
21. Jesus sends Peter and John to prepare the meal (Luke 22:8).
22. He shares his final meal with his disciples in a large upper room in a house in Jerusalem (Acts 12:12).

23. Afterwards, they leave the city, crossing the Kidron Valley to Gethsemane on the Mount of Olives (John 8:1).
24. Jesus spends the night in prayer.

Friday
25. 2:00 am – In the early hours of the morning, Jesus is betrayed and arrested in Gethsemane (John 18:1). He is taken to appear before Annas, the former high priest and is questioned (John 18:19).
26. Peter denies Jesus (John 18:15).
27. 3:00 am – Jesus is bound and sent to the high priest, Caiaphas (John 18:24). Peter denies him again (John 18:25).
28. Jesus is mocked and beaten. At sunrise he testifies that he is the Son of God and is led to Pilate. (Luke 22:66)
29. 6:00 am – Jesus is questioned by Pilate at Fort Antonia and sent to Herod's Palace in Jerusalem.
30. Jesus refuses to speak to Herod, and is sent back to Pilate in a mock royal robe (Luke 23:11).
31. Jesus is beaten and sentenced to be crucified (Matthew 27:27).
32. He carries the cross outside the walls of the city and is crucified.

THE LORD'S SUPPER

It was time for the Passover feast, and Jesus and his disciples had gathered for the meal. Jesus knew he would soon have to leave his friends. He was sad and troubled. "Soon, one of you will betray me," he said sorrowfully. The disciples looked at one another in shock. Who could he mean? But when Judas Iscariot left the room, none of them realized that he was the one Jesus was talking about.

Then Jesus handed around some bread, saying, "This is my body, which will be broken." Next, he passed around a cup of wine, saying, "Drink this. It is my blood, which will take away sin," and he told them he would soon be leaving them.

Simon Peter cried out, "But, Lord, why can't I follow you? I would lay down my life for you!"

"Would you, my friend?" asked Jesus gently. "And yet you will disown me three times before the cock crows!" Peter was horrified.

Matthew 26; Mark 14; Luke 22; John 13

Map 19
B5

IN THE GARDEN OF GETHSEMANE

Map 19
E2

Jesus and the disciples went to a quiet garden called Gethsemane. Jesus went aside to pray to for his disciples, and for all who would come to believe in him. Then he cried out, "Father, if it is possible, may I not have to go through this!" Yet his next words were, "Yet let it not be as I will, but as you will, Father," for Jesus knew that God wasn't making him do anything. He had chosen to do it.

He woke his friends, for they had fallen asleep. He knew the hour had come. At that moment a crowd of people burst into the garden, many armed with weapons. At the head of them was Judas Iscariot. Jesus said sadly, "Oh Judas, would you betray the Son of Man with a kiss?"

Peter drew his sword, but Jesus told him to put it away, and he allowed the soldiers to arrest him. "I'm the one you have come for," he said quietly. "Let these others go. You had no need to come here with swords and clubs."

When the disciples realized Jesus was going to allow himself to be taken, they fled in despair.

Matthew 26; Mark 14; Luke 22; John 17

A COCK CROWS

When the soldiers took Jesus to be questioned, Simon Peter followed them to the courtyard of the high priest. He waited outside miserably, along with the guards warming themselves at the fire. As one of the servant girls was walking by, she caught sight of Peter by the fire. "Weren't you with Jesus of Nazareth?" she asked him. "I'm sure I saw you with him."

Fearful of what would happen, Peter denied it vehemently, but then the girl asked one of the guards if he didn't look like one of Jesus' disciples.

"I don't have anything to do with him!" panicked Peter.

Another guard mentioned that he sounded as though he came from Galilee, and again Peter swore he didn't know Jesus. At that moment, a cock crowed. Peter remembered what Jesus had said, and he wept in dismay.

Matthew 26; Mark 14; Luke 22; John 18

PILATE WASHES HIS HANDS

Jesus was passed between the priests, the Roman governor Pontius Pilate, and even King Herod, but finally it fell to Pilate to decide his fate. During Passover it was the custom to release one prisoner. A man named Barabbas was in prison for rebellion and murder. Pilate called the priests and the people before him and asked who they wanted him to release. The crowd answered, "Barabbas!" for they had been told to say this.

"What shall I do with the one you call King of the Jews?" Pilate asked.

"Crucify him!" roared the crowd. When he asked for what crime, they only shouted louder.

Pilate didn't want to order the execution—but he didn't want a riot! He sent for a bowl of water and washed his hands to show that he took no responsibility for Jesus' death. Then he released Barabbas and had Jesus handed over to be crucified.

Matthew 27; Mark 15; Luke 23; John 18

Map 19
C2

MOCKED

Jesus was taken away by the soldiers. "Since you are the King of the Jews, let's dress you for the occasion!" they mocked, and they dressed him in a purple robe, the color worn by kings, and put a crown of thorny branches upon his head. Then they beat him and spat in his face before putting him back in his own clothes and leading him through the streets toward Golgotha, the place where he was to be crucified.

They made him carry the wooden cross on his back, but it was large and heavy, and Jesus had been dreadfully beaten. When he could do it no longer, they snatched someone from out of the crowd to carry it for him. And so the dreadful procession made its way out of the city to the hill of Golgotha.

Matthew 27; Mark 15; Luke 23; John 19

Map 19
B3

THE CRUCIFIXION

Soldiers nailed Jesus' hands and feet to the cross and placed above his head a sign saying, JESUS OF NAZARETH, KING OF THE JEWS. As they raised the cross, Jesus cried, "Father, forgive them. They don't know what they're doing."

Two thieves were crucified beside him. The first sneered at him, but the other said, "Be quiet! We deserve our punishment, but this man has done nothing wrong." Then he turned to Jesus and said, "Please remember me when you come into your kingdom," and Jesus promised he would be with him that day in Paradise.

The guards drew lots to see who would win Jesus' clothes, while the priests and Pharisees taunted him. "If you come down from the cross now, we'll believe in you!"

At midday, a shadow passed across the sun, and darkness fell over the land for three hours. At three o'clock, Jesus cried out, "My God, why have you forsaken me?" Then he gave a great cry, "It is finished!" and with these words, he gave up his spirit.

Matthew 27;
Mark 15;
Luke 23;
John 19

THE EMPTY TOMB

After Jesus was buried, the tomb was covered with a large stone, and Pilate placed guards there. Early on the first day of the week, Mary Magdalene and some other women went to anoint the body. As they came near to the tomb, the earth shook, the guards were thrown to the ground, and the women saw that the stone had been rolled away from the entrance. And inside the tomb, shining brighter than the sun, was an angel!

The angel said, "Why are you looking for the living among the dead? He is not here—he has risen! Don't you remember that he told you this would happen? Go and tell his disciples that he will meet them in Galilee as he promised."

So the women hurried away to tell the disciples the news, afraid yet filled with joy.

Matthew 28; Mark 16;
Luke 24; John 20

DOUBTING THOMAS

That same evening, Jesus appeared to the disciples. At first, they couldn't believe it. Was he a ghost? But he reassured them and showed them his scars. "Touch me and see," he said. "A ghost doesn't have flesh and bones!" Then he went on to explain the Scriptures to them, and they were filled with joy and wonder.

Thomas was not with the others, and when they tried to tell him about it, he couldn't believe them. "Unless I put my finger where the nails were and touch the wound in his side, I will not believe."

A week later, Thomas was with the disciples when suddenly Jesus was among them again. Turning to Thomas he said, "Put your finger in the wounds in my hands. Feel my side. Stop doubting and believe!"

Thomas was overcome with joy. Now he believed!

Jesus said, "You believed because you saw me yourself. How blessed will people be who believe without seeing!"

Luke 24; John 20

THE ASCENSION

Jesus and his friends were on a hillside outside Jerusalem. The time had come for Jesus to leave the world. In the time since his resurrection, he had made many things clearer to them and had told them a little about what the future would hold.

Jesus turned to his disciples. "You must stay here in Jerusalem for now and wait for the gift that my Father has promised you, for soon you will be baptized with the Holy Spirit. Then you must spread my message not only in Jerusalem and Judea and Samaria, but in every country."

He held up his hands to bless them and then, before their eyes, he was taken up to heaven, and a cloud hid him from sight.

As they stood looking upward in wonder, suddenly two men dressed in white stood beside them. "Why are you looking at the sky? Jesus has been taken from you into heaven, but he will come back again in the same way that he left!"

Mark 16; Luke 24; Acts 1

Map 19
E2

Spreading the Good News

THE HOLY SPIRIT

It was ten days since Jesus had been taken up to heaven. The twelve disciples (for they had chosen a replacement for Judas Iscariot) were gathered together when suddenly the house was filled with the sound of a mighty wind coming from heaven. As they watched in wonder, tongues of fire seemed to rest on each person there. They were all filled with the Holy Spirit and began to speak in different languages—languages they had never spoken before or studied!

Hearing the commotion, a huge crowd gathered outside. Great was their amazement when the disciples came out and began talking in different languages! Everyone there could hear the disciples explain the story of Jesus, whatever their nationality, and many came to believe because of that day.

Acts 2

Map 20 H5

THE LAME MAN

A lame man sat begging outside the temple gates. As Peter and John passed by on their way to pray, he looked up hopefully. "I don't have any money," Peter said. "But I can give you something far better! In the name of Jesus Christ, I order you to get up and walk!" and to everyone's astonishment, he helped him to stand up. The man tried a few cautious steps, and then a few more, and then walked straight into the temple to give thanks to God!

Peter explained to people that it was faith in the name of Jesus that had healed him. The authorities tried to stop the disciples, but they carried on talking about Jesus and passing on the good news.

Acts 3

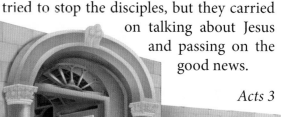

Saul became known by the Roman version of his name, Paul.

THE ROAD TO DAMASCUS

Saul hated the followers of Jesus. He wanted to put a stop to their preaching and believed he was doing God's will. Many Christians fled to avoid imprisonment, but they spread the word wherever they went. Knowing that many had gone to the city of Damascus, Saul set off in pursuit. Suddenly, a blinding light flashed down. Saul fell to the ground, covering his eyes. Then he heard a voice say, "Saul, why do you keep on persecuting me?"

Saul began trembling. He thought he knew who was speaking, but he had to ask, and the voice replied, "I am Jesus. Go into the city, and you will be told what you must do."

Saul struggled to his feet, but when he opened his eyes, he couldn't see a thing! His guards took him to the city where he spent three days in prayer. God sent a Christian to him, and when he laid his hands on Saul, it was as if scales had fallen from his eyes! Saul arose and was baptized.

Saul began to spread the good news about Jesus and people were amazed, for he had once been the greatest enemy of the Christians. He went on to become one of the greatest of all the apostles.

Acts 9

Map 20 H4

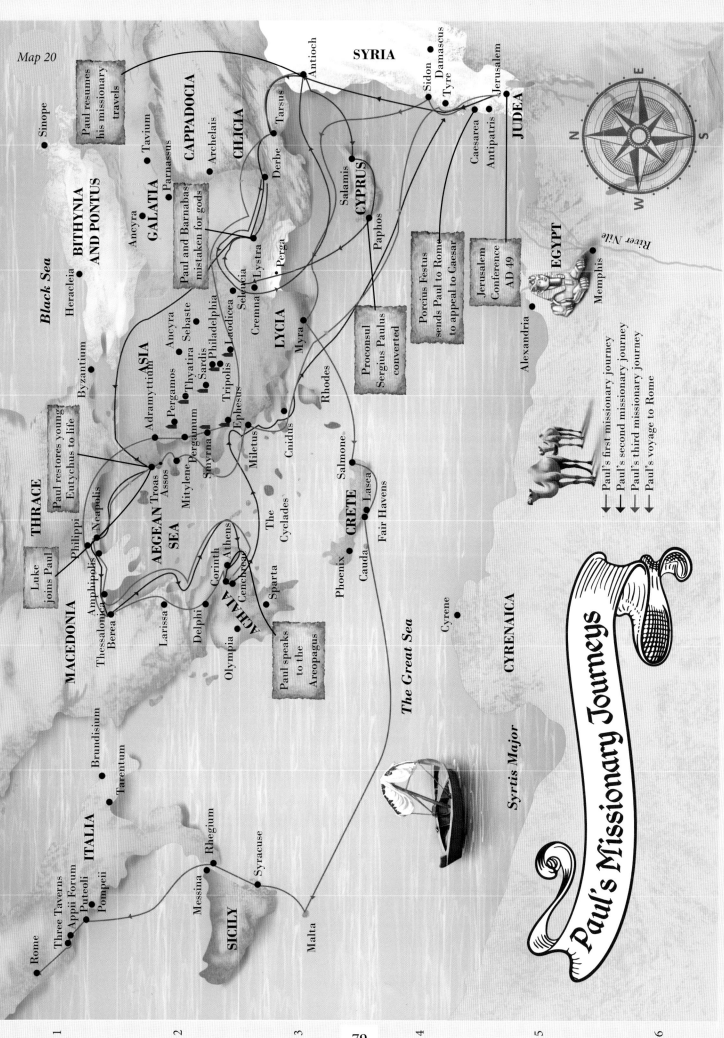

Map 20

SYRIA

Black Sea

BITHYNIA AND PONTUS

CAPPADOCIA

GALATIA

CILICIA

CYPRUS

JUDEA

EGYPT

River Nile

THRACE

ASIA

LYCIA

MACEDONIA

ACHAIA

AEGEAN SEA

CRETE

The Great Sea

CYRENAICA

Syrtis Major

ITALIA

SICILY

Paul resumes his missionary travels

Paul and Barnabas mistaken for gods

Proconsul Sergius Paulus converted

Porcius Festus sends Paul to Rome to appeal to Caesar

Jerusalem Conference AD 49

Paul restores young Eutychus to life

Luke joins Paul

Paul speaks to the Areopagus

Sinope
Heracleia
Byzantium
Tavium
Ancyra
Parnassus
Archelais
Tarsus
Antioch
Sidon
Damascus
Tyre
Jerusalem
Caesarea
Antipatris
Derbe
Salamis
Paphos
Ancyra
Pergamos
Thyatira
Sardis
Philadelphia
Laodicea
Seleucia
Lystra
Perga
Myra
Rhodes
Adramyttium
Sebaste
Tripolis
Ephesus
Smyrna
Pergamum
Miletus
Cnidus
Salmone
Memphis
Alexandria
Philippi
Neapolis
Troas
Assos
Mitylene
Athens
Corinth
Cenchrea
Sparta
The Cyclades
Phoenix
Cauda
Lasea
Fair Havens
Amphipolis
Thessalonica
Berea
Larissa
Delphi
Olympia
Cyrene
Rome
Three Taverns
Appii Forum
Puteoli
Pompeii
Brundisium
Tarentum
Rhegium
Messina
Syracuse
Malta

⇩ Paul's first missionary journey
⇩ Paul's second missionary journey
⇩ Paul's third missionary journey
⇩ Paul's voyage to Rome

Paul's Missionary Journeys

1
2
3
4
5
6

STRUCK BLIND

God told Paul and another man named Barnabas to go on a journey to spread the good news to people who had not yet heard about Jesus. They went first to Cyprus, where they converted the Roman governor after Paul rebuked the evil sorcerer Elymas.

From Cyprus they traveled to Perga in modern-day Turkey, and then through difficult countryside into the heart of Anatolia. Wherever they went they relied on the hospitality of the local people and spoke about Jesus to both Jews and Gentiles.

Acts 13

Map 21
G4

SINGING IN PRISON

On Paul's second missionary journey, he and his friend Silas had been thrown into prison in Philippi. It was midnight and Paul and Silas were lying in the stocks—praying and singing hymns! The other prisoners could hardly believe their ears.

Suddenly a violent earthquake shook the cell doors open, and everyone's chains came loose! Paul called out to the terrified jailor, "Don't worry! We're still here!" The jailor took Paul and Silas to his house, where he and his family spent the night learning about Jesus. They became Christians that night!

After this, Paul traveled on through many lands to tell people his wonderful message. He spent time in Athens and in Corinth. Then he traveled to Ephesus and Caesarea before settling for a while in Antioch at the end of his second missionary journey.

Acts 16

Map 21
D1

TAKEN FOR GODS

From Anatolia, Paul and Barnabas traveled to Lystra, where Paul healed a lame man. The excited crowd believed that he and Barnabas were gods! The priest of Zeus brought bulls and wreaths to the city gates because he and the crowd wanted to offer sacrifices to the apostles! They had a hard job explaining that they were ordinary men and trying to tell them about God!

Soon after, some Jews turned the people against the apostles. They stoned Paul and left him for dead outside the city, but after the disciples had gathered around, he got up and went back to preach as if nothing had happened.

Next, Paul and Barnabas visited the city of Derbe before making their way back to Antioch, stopping along the way to encourage those they had already spoken to and help as they set up new churches.

Acts 14

Map 21
G3

RIOT AT EPHESUS

Paul was in Ephesus, on the third of his missionary journeys, when trouble erupted. The people there worshipped the goddess Artemis and had built a wonderful temple in her honor. People came from afar to visit it, and the city was full of silversmiths selling silver images of the goddess. But when Paul started preaching, many people became Christians and stopped buying the images. The silversmiths were furious, and soon the whole city was in an uproar!

Paul realized that it would be safer for everyone if he left the city, and so he set off to return to Jerusalem, heading first to Macedonia and then Greece.

Acts 19

Map 21
E2

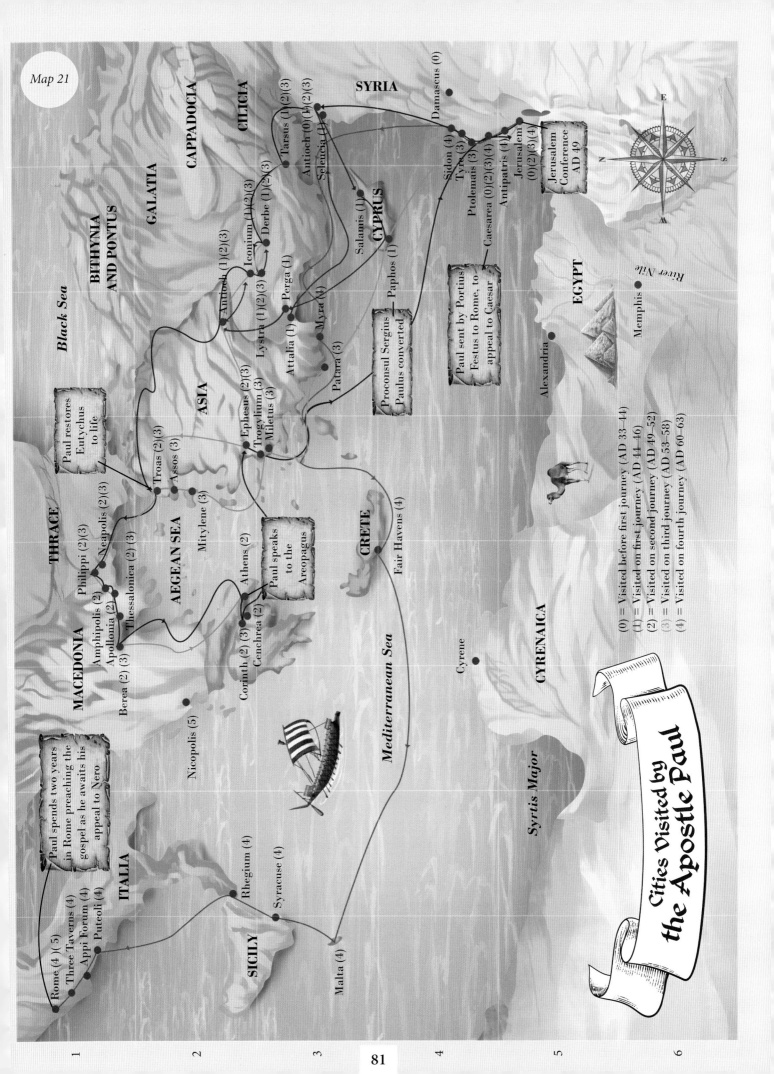

Map 21

Cities Visited by the Apostle Paul

SYRIA
Damascus (0)
Tarsus (1)(2)(3)
Antioch (0)(1)(2)(3)
Seleucia (1)
CILICIA
CAPPADOCIA
GALATIA
BITHYNIA AND PONTUS
Black Sea
Antioch (1)(2)(3)
Iconium (1)(2)(3)
Derbe (1)(2)(3)
Lystra (1)(2)(3)
Perga (1)
Attalia (1)
Myra (4)
Patara (3)
Salamis (1)
CYPRUS
Paphos (1)

Sidon (4)
Tyre (3)
Ptolemais (3)
Caesarea (0)(2)(3)(4)
Antipatris (4)
Jerusalem (0)(2)(3)(4)

Jerusalem Conference AD 49

Proconsul Sergius Paulus converted

Paul sent by Portius Festus to Rome, to appeal to Caesar

EGYPT
Alexandria
Memphis
River Nile

ASIA
Ephesus (2)(3)
Trogylium (3)
Miletus (3)
Troas (2)(3)
Assos (3)
Mitylene (3)

THRACE
MACEDONIA
Philippi (2)(3)
Neapolis (2)(3)
Amphipolis (2)
Apollonia (2)
Thessalonica (2) (3)
Berea (2)(3)

Paul restores Eutychus to life

AEGEAN SEA
Athens (2)
Corinth (2) (3)
Cenchrea (2)

Paul speaks to the Areopagus

CRETE
Fair Havens (4)

Nicopolis (5)

Mediterranean Sea

Cyrene
CYRENAICA
Syrtis Major

ITALIA
Rome (4) (5)
Three Taverns (4)
Appi Forum (4)
Puteoli (4)

Paul spends two years in Rome preaching the gospel as he awaits his appeal to Nero

SICILY
Rhegium (4)
Syracuse (4)

Malta (4)

(0) = Visited before first journey (AD 33–44)
(1) = Visited on first journey (AD 44–46)
(2) = Visited on second journey (AD 49–52)
(3) = Visited on third journey (AD 53–58)
(4) = Visited on fourth journey (AD 60–63)

1

2

3

4

5

6

"PLEASE DON'T GO!"

Paul wanted to return to Jerusalem to help the Jewish Christians there. His friends didn't want him to go—they feared that he would be imprisoned there and probably killed.

But Paul shook his head sadly. "Please don't try to change my mind with your tears. This is what I have to do. I'm ready not only to be put in chains for Jesus, but to die for him."

Even though he knew in his heart that hardship and suffering were ahead of him, Paul would go where God wanted him to go. Before he boarded the ship that would carry him onward, Paul knelt with his friends and prayed. They all wept as he sailed away. They knew that they would never see him again.

Acts 20

Map 21
E2

TROUBLE IN JERUSALEM

Paul received a warm welcome from his friends in Jerusalem, but trouble soon flared up. Many Jews didn't like the message he was preaching. When they came upon Paul in the temple, they stirred the crowd up and told lies about him. The crowd dragged him from the temple, and he would probably have been killed if it hadn't been for the Roman governor of the city, who learned about the uproar and sent in troops.

The commander tried to find out what Paul had done, but one person shouted one thing, and another screamed something else, and there was so much uproar that the commander thought he had better get Paul out of there quickly and into the barracks. The soldiers had to lift him up to stop the crowd from getting to him!

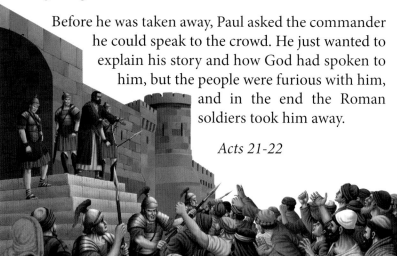

Before he was taken away, Paul asked the commander he could speak to the crowd. He just wanted to explain his story and how God had spoken to him, but the people were furious with him, and in the end the Roman soldiers took him away.

Acts 21-22

Map 22
H5

CONSPIRACY

The Roman commander wanted to find out exactly what Paul was being accused of, so he sent him before the chief priests and the Jewish council, but they only argued among themselves, and Paul was sent back. But some of the Jews hated Paul so much that they planned to murder him. Paul's nephew heard about the plot and told the commander, who smuggled Paul out of the city under cover of darkness.

Some days later, Paul found himself in Caesarea. His enemies told the Roman governor that Paul was a trouble-maker who had stirred up riots. They claimed he was the ringleader of the Nazarene sect and that he had tried to desecrate the temple at Jerusalem. When Paul was allowed to speak, he explained that the accusations were false. The governor knew that Paul's accusers could prove nothing but still kept Paul under guard, as did the governor after him. In the end, Paul demanded that his case be heard by the emperor in Rome. Festus first sent him to be questioned by King Agrippa, who could only say that if Paul hadn't already demanded to go to Rome, then surely he should have been set free. As it was, to Rome he must go.

Acts 22-26

Map 22

Paul Travels to Rome

Tarsus
Antioch
Sidon
Tyre
Caesarea
Antipatris
Jerusalem

CYPRUS
Salamis
Paphos

Portius Festus sends Paul to Rome to appeal to Caesar

EGYPT

Alexandria

Perga
Myra
Attalia

Change to a larger grain ship

The Great Sea

Adramyttium

Ephesus
Trogylium
Miletus
Cnidus

Aegean Sea

Mitylene

CRETE
Lasea
Phoenix
Fair Havens

Athens

Corinth
Cenchrea

CYRENAICA

Cyrene

Ship lost in storm

Nicopolis

Adriatic Sea

Paul spends two years preaching the gospel while he awaits his appeal to Ceasar

ITALIA

Rome
Three Taverns
Appi Forum
Puteoli

Rhegium

Syracuse

SICILY

Malta

Ship smashes into reef. Everyone swims to shore.

Syrtis Major

N E S W

83

STORM AT SEA

Paul was traveling to Rome aboard a ship. Julius, the Roman centurion in charge, took a liking to Paul and treated him kindly. However, bad weather and stops delayed their voyage, and the stormy season was upon them. When they lay at anchor at a harbor in Crete, Paul warned Julius and the captain that it would be dangerous to sail onward. But the captain ignored him and set sail.

Soon they found themselves in a dreadful storm. For days the ship was at the mercy of the sea. The crew began throwing cargo over the side to try to save the ship, and after several days passed without sight of the sun or stars, all hope seemed lost.

Then Paul spoke to the crew and passengers to give them comfort. "Keep up your courage because an angel has spoken to me and has promised we will all reach land alive. Only the ship will be lost. Have faith in God as I do. We will be saved."

Acts 27

*Map 22
C4*

SHIPWRECKED!

After two weeks at the mercy of the storm, they reached shallower waters. Some tried to leave in a lifeboat, as they feared that they would be dashed upon the rocks, but Paul told the captain and the centurion that they must all to stay with the ship to be saved.

Just before dawn Paul urged them all to eat. He took some bread himself and, thanking God, began to eat, and so the other passengers were encouraged to eat too.

Just as the coastline finally came into sight, suddenly the ship struck a sandbar. The bow stuck fast, and the ship began to be broken to pieces by the surf!

The soldiers planned to kill the prisoners to prevent any from swimming away and escaping, but Julius ordered all who could swim to make for land, and he told those who could not swim to cling to pieces of the wreckage and float ashore. In this way, everyone reached land safely. Every last one of the two hundred and seventy-six people on board was saved, just as God had promised!

Acts 27

*Map 22
A3*

ROME AT LAST

Paul and his companions found themselves on the island of Malta. They were cold and wet, but they were alive! Some islanders came to help. They lit a huge fire to warm them. While Paul was putting some extra wood on the fire, a poisonous snake slithered out and fastened itself on his hand. Paul calmly shook the snake off and carried on as if nothing had happened. The astonished islanders thought he must be a god!

After three months, they set sail once again for Rome. While he waited for his case to be heard, Paul was allowed to live by himself with a soldier to guard him. Although he was not allowed out, he could have visitors, and so he was able to carry on spreading the message to new people. He also wrote letters to the Christians he had met during his travels, to encourage and help them as they set up their churches. It is not known for sure how Paul died, but many believe that he was executed while in Rome.

Acts 28

*Map 22
A1*

THE LOVE OF GOD

Paul's letters and others make up a large portion of the New Testament. They speak to us even today, for many of the problems we face and the fears we have are the same, the advice is still relevant, and the comfort offered is as true as ever.

Paul wrote to the believers in Rome before he went to the city. His words helped to explain how our faith in Jesus Christ will save us. We can't save ourselves from our sins, but God, in his loving kindness, sent us his Son so that we could be saved by accepting Jesus as our Savior.

Paul wrote that life will be hard, but that we will be rewarded in the end: "I believe our present suffering is not worth comparing with the glory that will be revealed in us—and suffering produces perseverance, character, and hope!"

Romans 8

Map 23 C3

PUT ON GOD'S ARMOR

Paul told the people of the church in Ephesus: "Be strong in the Lord. Our enemies aren't made of flesh and blood, so put on every piece of God's armour. Then you can stand firm, with the belt of truth buckled round your waist, and the breastplate of righteousness on your chest. Let your feet be shod with the readiness that comes from the gospel of peace, and take up the shield of faith. Put on the helmet of salvation, and take hold of the sword of the Spirit, which is the word of God."

God's word and God's love are our protection against all that life can throw at us.

Ephesians 6

Map 23 F4

THE GREATEST OF THESE

To the Corinthians, Paul wrote, "If I could speak every language and talk with angels, but didn't love others, I would be no more than a noisy gong. If I had the gift of prophecy, or knowledge, or such great faith that I could move mountains, it would mean nothing if I didn't have love. I could give all I owned to the poor, but it would be meaningless if I didn't feel love for the people.

"Love is patient and kind. It isn't jealous, boastful, proud, or rude. It doesn't insist on having its own way, or become irritable, or seek revenge. Love protects, and trusts, and hopes. It is steady and true, and it never, ever gives up. Three things will last forever—faith, hope, and love—and the greatest of these is love."

1 Corinthians 13

Map 23 E4

A GOOD FIGHT

Toward the end of his life, Paul wrote to Timothy: "I am suffering and have been chained like a criminal, but the word of God cannot be chained. Remind everyone:

"'If we die with him, we will also live with him.
If we endure hardship, we will reign with him.
If we deny him, he will deny us.
If we are unfaithful, he remains faithful,
for he cannot deny who he is.'

Map 23 C3

"The time of my death is near. I have fought a good fight, I have finished the race, and I have kept the faith. Now I look forward to my reward, which the Lord will give me on the day of his return—a reward not just for me but for all who eagerly await his coming!"

2 Timothy

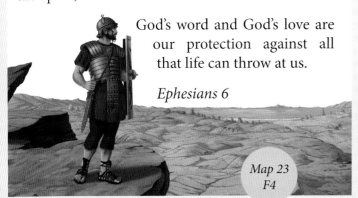

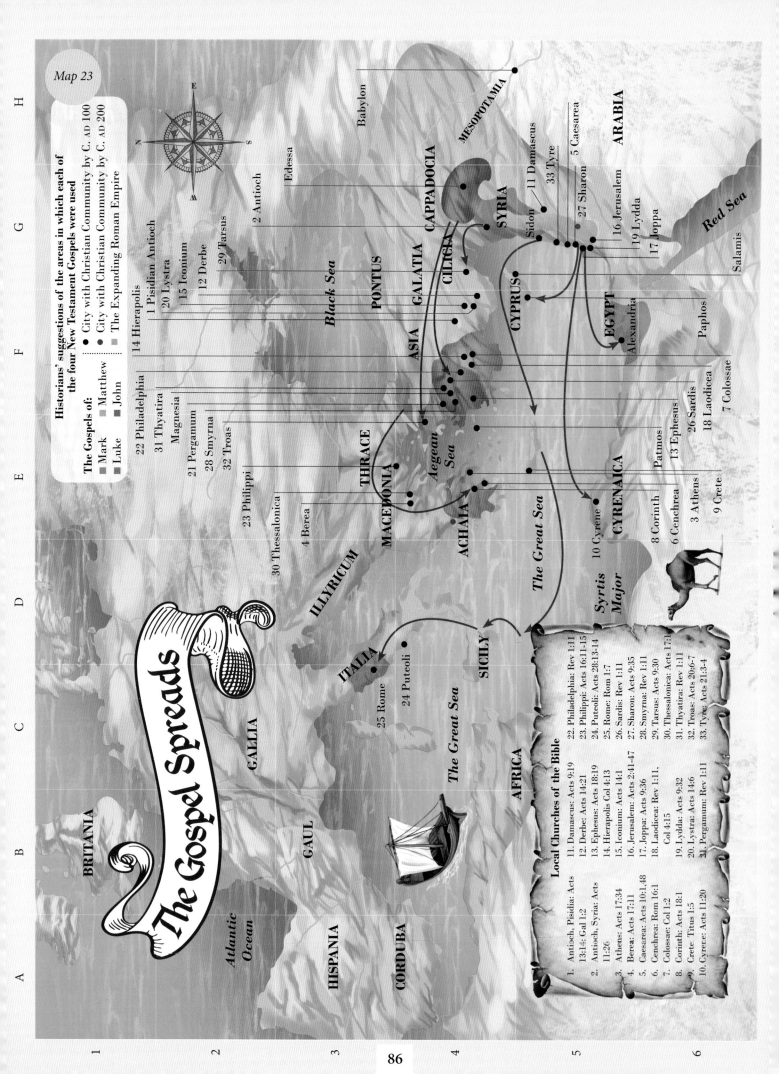

The Gospel Spreads

Map 23

Historians' suggestions of the areas in which each of
the four New Testament Gospels were used

● City with Christian Community by C. AD 100
◐ City with Christian Community by C. AD 200
▨ The Expanding Roman Empire

The Gospels of:
Mark   Matthew
Luke   John

Local Churches of the Bible

1. Antioch, Pisidia: Acts 13:14; Gal 1:2
2. Antioch, Syria: Acts 11:26
3. Athens: Acts 17:34
4. Berea: Acts 17:11
5. Caesarea: Acts 10:1,48
6. Cenchrea: Rom 16:1
7. Colossae: Col 1:2
8. Corinth: Acts 18:1
9. Crete: Titus 1:5
10. Cyrene: Acts 11:20
11. Damascus: Acts 9:19
12. Derbe: Acts 14:21
13. Ephesus: Acts 18:19
14. Hierapolis Col 4:13
15. Iconium: Acts 14:1
16. Jerusalem: Acts 2:41-47
17. Joppa: Acts 9:36
18. Laodicea: Rev 1:11, Col 4:15
19. Lydda: Acts 9:32
20. Lystra: Acts 14:6
21. Pergamum: Rev 1:11
22. Philadelphia: Rev 1:11
23. Philippi: Acts 16:11-15
24. Puteoli: Acts 28:13-14
25. Rome: Rom 1:7
26. Sardis: Rev 1:11
27. Sharon: Acts 9:35
28. Smyrna: Rev 1:11
29. Tarsus: Acts 9:30
30. Thessalonica: Acts 17:1
31. Thyatira: Rev 1:11
32. Troas: Acts 20:6-7
33. Tyre: Acts 21:3-4

BRITANIA
GALLIA
GAUL
HISPANIA
CORDUBA
Atlantic Ocean

ITALIA
25 Rome
24 Puteoli
SICILY
The Great Sea
AFRICA
Syrtis Major
CYRENAICA
10 Cyrene

ILLYRICUM
THRACE
MACEDONIA
30 Thessalonica
4 Berea
23 Philippi
Aegean Sea
ACHAIA
8 Corinth
6 Cenchrea
3 Athens
9 Crete
Patmos
13 Ephesus
18 Laodicea
7 Colossae
26 Sardis

Black Sea
PONTUS
GALATIA
ASIA
14 Hierapolis
22 Philadelphia
31 Thyatira
Magnesia
21 Pergamum
28 Smyrna
32 Troas
1 Pisidian Antioch
20 Lystra
15 Iconium
12 Derbe
29 Tarsus
CAPPADOCIA
CILICIA
2 Antioch
Edessa
Babylon
MESOPOTAMIA

CYPRUS
Paphos
Salamis
SYRIA
Sidon
11 Damascus
33 Tyre
5 Caesarea
27 Sharon
16 Jerusalem
19 Lydda
17 Joppa
ARABIA
EGYPT
Alexandria
Red Sea
The Great Sea

86

RUN THE RACE

We cannot be certain who wrote the book of Hebrews, although some believe it might have been Paul. In Hebrews we're told, "Faith is the confidence that what we hope for will actually happen. Our ancestors had faith: Noah built a boat when everyone was laughing at him; Sarah believed she would have a child even though she was old; Moses took his people out of Egypt just because God told him to. Let yourself be filled with faith. Cast off the things that weigh you down so you have the strength and endurance to run the race set before us!"

The writer knew that our Christian journey would not be an easy one, but if we depend on Jesus for help, we will grow stronger.

Hebrews

REAL FAITH

Other writers also had inspiring words to say about faith. The apostle James wrote, "What good is it to say you have faith but don't show it by your actions? Words are not enough—faith is not enough unless it produces good deeds." James told his readers that they should ask God for the things they needed, but that when they asked, they really had to believe and not doubt. If you doubt, then you are like "a wave of the sea, blown and tossed by the wind."

Peter wrote, "You face hardship and suffering—but don't despair! Instead, be glad, for these trials make you partners with Christ in his suffering. They will test your faith as fire tests and purifies gold, and remember that there is wonderful joy ahead! Don't be disheartened if it seems a long time in coming—God is being patient, for he wants everyone to repent. But the day of the Lord will come unexpectedly, so be prepared!

James; 1-2 Peter

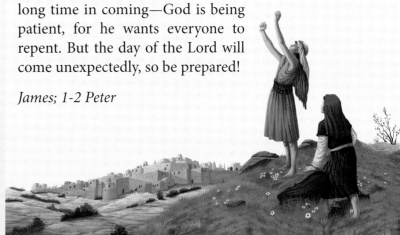

GOD IS LOVE

The apostle John wrote, "God is love. He showed how much he loved us by sending his one and only Son into the world so that we might have eternal life through him. Since he loved us that much, let us make sure that we love one another so that God can live in us and we can live in God. And as we live in God, our love will grow more perfect, and when the day of judgment comes we will not have to fear anything. Perfect love drives out all fear! We love one another because he loved us first."

1 John

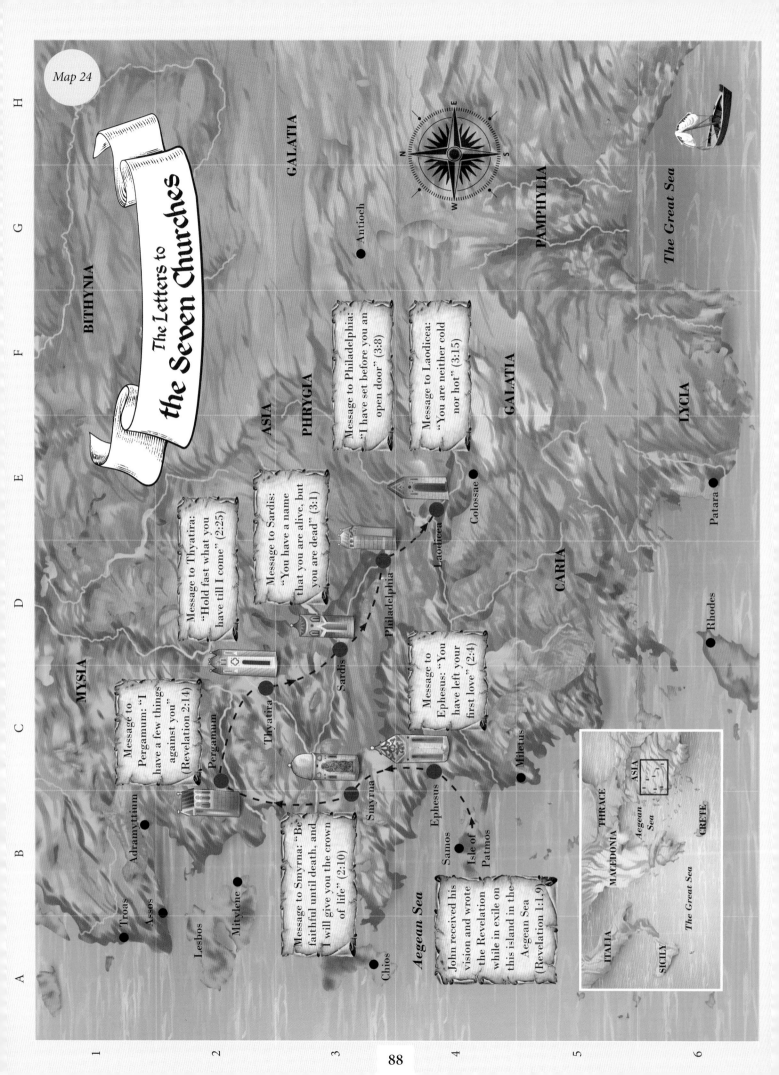

Map 24

The Letters to the Seven Churches

BITHYNIA

GALATIA

GALATIA

PHRYGIA

ASIA

MYSIA

CARIA

LYCIA

PAMPHYLIA

The Great Sea

Antioch

Message to Philadelphia: "I have set before you an open door" (3:8)

Message to Laodicea: "You are neither cold nor hot" (3:15)

Message to Thyatira: "Hold fast what you have till I come" (2:25)

Message to Sardis: "You have a name that you are alive, but you are dead" (3:1)

Message to Pergamum: "I have a few things against you" (Revelation 2:14)

Message to Ephesus: "You have left your first love" (2:4)

Message to Smyrna: "Be faithful until death, and I will give you the crown of life" (2:10)

Colossae

Laodicea

Philadelphia

Sardis

Thyatira

Pergamum

Smyrna

Miletus

Ephesus

Patara

Rhodes

Adramyttium

Troas

Assos

Lesbos

Mitylene

Chios

Samos

Isle of Patmos

Aegean Sea

John received his vision and wrote the Revelation while in exile on this island in the Aegean Sea (Revelation 1:9)

THRACE

MACEDONIA

ITALIA

SICILY

ASIA

Aegean Sea

CRETE

The Great Sea

The very last book of the Bible is Revelation. Many believe it was written by the disciple John on the island of Patmos. The author had an amazing vision to pass on: "On the Lord's day the Spirit took control of me, and I heard a loud voice coming from behind me, saying, 'Write down what you see and send it to the seven churches.'

"When I turned, I saw seven golden lampstands, and among them I saw a being like the Son of Man. His head and hair were white as snow, and his eyes were like blazing fire. In his right hand he held seven stars, and out of his mouth came a sharp double-edged sword. His face shone like the brightest sun. 'I am the First and the Last,' he said. 'I was dead, and behold I am alive for ever and ever! And I hold the keys of death and Hades.'"

In John's vision, the seven lampstands were the seven churches of Asia Minor, and the Lord wanted John to send a message to those churches, to correct and encourage them.

Revelation 1

Map 24
B4

LETTERS TO THE SEVEN CHURCHES

John was told to write to the people of the seven churches of Asia Minor. Each church faced challenges: The church at Ephesus was doing good works but had gone off track in its relationship with Christ; the church at Smyrna was keeping faith but was under persecution; the church at Pergamum was faithful but was listening to false teachers; the church at Thyatira had come a long way but was still tolerating a false prophetess; the church of Sardis was spiritually dead and needed to wake up; the church at Philadelphia was faithful but small; and the church at Laodicea was nothing more than lukewarm—they were materially rich but failed to realize that spiritually they were poor.

Jesus wanted the people of these churches to look within themselves and truly repent and welcome him into their hearts. The letters were a warning, but they were also a promise.

Revelation 2-3

Map 24

"I'M COMING SOON!"

John saw many dreadful things in his vision. A terrible time was to follow, but finally all that is evil will be destroyed, and God's kingdom will reign. After the final judgment, a new heaven and earth will replace the old.

He wrote, "Then I saw a new heaven and earth, and I saw the Holy City coming down out of heaven like a beautiful bride. I heard a loud voice speaking from the throne: 'Now God's home is with his people! He will live with them. They shall be his people, and he will be their God. There will be no more death, no more grief, or crying, or pain. He will make all things new! For he is the first and the last, the beginning and the end.'

"And I was shown the Holy City, shining with the glory of God. Its temple is the Lord God Almighty and the Lamb. But only those whose names are written in the Lamb's Book of Life will enter.

"'Listen!' says Jesus. 'I'm coming soon!'"

Amen. Come, Lord Jesus.

Revelation 21-22

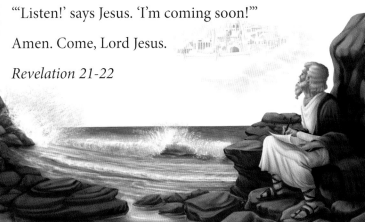